"If you want to move to another level in your spiritual life and leadership, take the time to read this book. It is not just biblical, but practical and readable. The emphasis on the local church and its role in discipling others sets it apart from other books. Read it and share it with others."

Ronnie Floyd, President and CEO, Executive Committee, The Southern Baptist Convention; Pastor Emeritus, Cross Church, Springdale, Arkansas

"Mark Dever is known for being a faithful, exegetical preacher of God's Word. But what you may not know is that Mark is an intentional disciple-maker. Whether he's meeting on Saturday with lay leaders over lunch to discuss his application grid for Sunday's message or discussing church polity in his study with a group of young interns, Mark emulates what he expects from others. I believe his legacy will not be just on the pages of the books he has penned, but on the hearts of the men he's invested in personally. Don't just read this book. Implement the biblical principles found within."

Robby Gallaty, Senior Pastor, Long Hollow Baptist Church, Hendersonville, Tennessee

"I love reading books written by authors who are zealous about the subjects they write about. I often feel like emulating their example even before I get to the last page of the book. If you know Mark Dever, then you know he is a committed discipler. Discipleship oozes out of him. What drives him and how he disciples others and gets his church members to do the same is what these pages are all about. Prepare yourself for a life-changing experience as you read this book!"

Conrad Mwebe, Pastor, Kabwata Baptist Church, Lusaka, Zambia

"This book convicts, exhorts, and instructs followers of Christ concerning the call to a life of discipling others. It also offers warm-hearted glimpses of this call being answered in the life of a pastor and his congregation. Mark Dever takes us to the Scriptures and roots us in the church, with particular focus on church leaders and careful attention to all. This makes much sense, but we need to be reminded that the process of discipling others is every believer's clear and joyful calling."

Kathleen B. Nielson, Former Director of Women's Initiatives, The Gospel Coalition

"With simple yet profound insights, Mark Dever takes Jesus's final command to make disciples and teaches us what that means for us and for our churches. By answering our questions—the why, the what, the where, and the how of discipling—Pastor Mark coaches us in how to follow Christ by helping others to follow him, to know the truth, and to live it well. Every follower of Christ needs to read this book! It's the best book I've ever read on discipling."

Jani Ortlund, Executive Vice President, Renewal Ministries; author, *Fearlessly Feminine* and *His Loving Law, Our Lasting Legacy*

"Here is a church-strengthening book full of down-to-earth advice about the nuts and bolts of discipling. Dever's love for Jesus and his people shines throughout, and his firm placement of discipleship within the context and bounds of the local church is vintage Dever ecclesiology. He has a keen eye for pastors, addressing them about their role with warmth and clarity. I was personally challenged by Dever, who himself has a track record of prioritizing discipleship in the midst of all his other responsibilities. If Mark does it, I can do it!"

Grant J. Retief, Senior Pastor, Christ Church, Umhlanga, Durban, South Africa

"Dever reminds readers that discipling is a biblical mandate, motivated by obedience to Christ's commandment and love for others, and it is not an effort reserved for a select few. It doesn't reduce people to projects, but rather it seeks to intentionally develop a relationship with them. It requires time invested in the lives of people who are interested and motivated to follow Jesus. Finally, only truly humble teachers should disciple Jesus's sheep, because 'when a disciple is fully trained, he will be like his teacher.' These emphases and more are contained within this book. Upon reading it, you will most likely recommend it to others. I know I will."

Miguel Núñez, Senior Pastor, International Baptist Church, Santo Domingo, Dominican Republic; President, Wisdom & Integrity Ministries

DISCIPLING

9Marks: Building Healthy Churches

Edited by Mark Dever and Jonathan Leeman

Biblical Theology: How the Church Faithfully Teaches the Gospel,
Nick Roark and Robert Cline

Church Elders: How to Shepherd God's People Like Jesus,
Jeramie Rinne

Church Discipline: How the Church Protects the Name of Jesus,
Jonathan Leeman

Church Membership: How the World Knows Who Represents Jesus, Jonathan Leeman

Conversion: How God Creates a People, Michael Lawrence

Discipling: How to Help Others Follow Jesus, Mark Dever

Evangelism: How the Whole Church Speaks of Jesus,
J. Mack Stiles

Expositional Preaching: How We Speak God's Word Today,
David Helm

The Gospel: How the Church Portrays the Beauty of Christ,
Ray Ortlund

Missions: How the Local Church Goes Global, Andy Johnson

Prayer: How Praying Together Shapes the Church,
John Onwuchekwa

Sound Doctrine: How a Church Grows in the Love and Holiness of God, Bobby Jamieson

BUILDING HEALTHY CHURCHES

DISCIPLING

HOW
TO HELP
OTHERS
FOLLOW
JESUS

MARK DEVER

WHEATON, ILLINOIS

Discipling: How to Help Others Follow Jesus

Copyright © 2016 by Mark Dever

Published by Crossway
        1300 Crescent Street
        Wheaton, Illinois 60187

Cover design: Dual Identity, inc.

Cover image: Wayne Brezinka for brezinkadesign.com

First printing 2016

Printed in the United States of America

Unless otherwise indicated, Scripture quotations are from the ESV® Bible (The Holy Bible, English Standard Version®), copyright © 2001 by Crossway, a publishing ministry of Good News Publishers. Used by permission. All rights reserved.

Scripture references marked NIV are taken from The Holy Bible, New International Version®, NIV®. Copyright © 1973, 1978, 1984, 2011 by Biblica, Inc.™ Used by permission. All rights reserved worldwide.

Trade Hardcover ISBN: 978-1-4335-5122-2
ePub ISBN: 978-1-4335-5125-3
PDF ISBN: 978-1-4335-5123-9
Mobipocket ISBN: 978-1-4335-5124-6

Library of Congress Cataloging-in-Publication Data

Dever, Mark.
    Discipling : how to help others follow Jesus / Mark Dever.
        pages cm.—(9Marks: building healthy churches)
        Includes bibliographical references and index.
        ISBN 978-1-4335-5122-2 (hc)
    1. Discipling (Christianity) I. Title.
BV4520.D44   2016
253—dc23   2015031755

Crossway is a publishing ministry of Good News Publishers.

LB		29	28	27	26	25	24	23	22	21	20	19
19	18	17	16	15	14	13	12	11	10	9	8	7

CONTENTS

Series Preface   9

Introduction   11

PART 1: WHAT IS DISCIPLING?

1   The Inevitability of Influence   23

2   Oriented toward Others   27

3   The Work of Discipling   35

4   Objections to Discipling   45

PART 2: WHERE SHOULD WE DISCIPLE?

5   The Local Church   51

6   Pastors and Members   59

PART 3: HOW SHOULD WE DISCIPLE?

7   Choose Someone   73

8   Have Clear Aims   83

9   Pay the Cost   87

10 Raising Up Leaders   93

Conclusion *by Jonathan Leeman*   105

Appendix: Books besides the Bible to Use in   115
      Discipling Relationships

Notes   119

Scripture Index   121

SERIES PREFACE

The 9Marks series of books is premised on two basic ideas. First, the local church is far more important to the Christian life than many Christians today perhaps realize.

Second, local churches grow in life and vitality as they organize their lives around God's Word. God speaks. Churches should listen and follow. It's that simple. When a church listens and follows, it begins to look like the One it is following. It reflects his love and holiness. It displays his glory. A church will look like him as it listens to him.

So our basic message to churches is, don't look to the best business practices or the latest styles; look to God. Start by listening to God's Word again.

Out of this overall project comes the 9Marks series of books. Some target pastors. Some target church members. Hopefully all will combine careful biblical examination, theological reflection, cultural consideration, corporate application, and even a bit of individual exhortation. The best Christian books are always both theological and practical.

It's our prayer that God will use this volume and the others to help prepare his bride, the church, with radiance and splendor for the day of his coming.

INTRODUCTION

For years my wife has had to endure my reluctance to ask for directions. You see, I know myself to be gifted with a natural sense of direction! Of course, that means my confidence sometimes outpaces my knowledge of the right way. As she says about me, "Always confident, sometimes right."

I am not alone in wanting to plow my own furrow. People love Robert Frost's words, "Two roads diverged in a wood, and I—I took the one less traveled by, and that has made all the difference." Henry David Thoreau remarked, "If a man does not keep pace with his companions, perhaps it is because he hears a different drummer." And William Ernest Henley famously declared, "I am the master of my fate: I am the captain of my soul."

It's not just the poets and writers who love their independence. The population at large is disengaging from their clubs, civic associations, and local churches, says Robert Putnam in *Bowling Alone*. The now-common sight of family members texting friends while ignoring each other at the dinner table explains Sherry Turkle's title *Alone Together: Why We Expect More from Technology and Less from Each Other*. And more and more people are choosing to live alone, notes Eric Klinenberg in *Going Solo*.[1]

Klinenberg writes,

In 1950, for instance, only 4 million Americans lived alone, and they accounted for less than 10 percent of all households. Today, more than 32 million Americans are going solo. They represent 28 percent of all households at the national level; more than 40 percent in cities including San Francisco, Seattle, Atlanta, Denver, and Minneapolis; and nearly 50 percent in Washington D.C. and Manhattan, the twin capitals of the solo nation.[2]

And this trend is not only in America. In Stockholm, Sweden, 60 percent of all households have just one occupant, according to Klinenberg.[3]

What's going on? Klinenberg finds that in many places residents increasingly value space less and nearness to amenities—stores, restaurants, and gyms—more. The singletons, as he calls them, are reshaping everything to be more convenient to them. Communal commitments, however, must be detachable and temporary.

Today is the day of iPhones and iPads, iTunes and—let's just say—the whole i-life. But is there any space in the i-life for the *we*-life of Christianity?

At the heart of Christianity is God's desire for a people to display his character. They do this through their obedience to his Word in their relationships with him and with each other. Therefore he sent his Son to call out a people to follow him. And part of following the Son is calling still more to follow the Son. Then, in their life together, these people display the *we*-life of the Father, Son, and Spirit. Together they demonstrate God's own love, holiness, and oneness.

His Son therefore gave this last command before ascending to heaven: *go and make disciples* (Matt. 28:19). The lives of these people, in other words, should be dedicated to helping others follow Jesus.

That's the working definition of *discipling* for this book: helping others to follow Jesus. You can see it in the subtitle. Another way we could define discipling might be: discipling is deliberately doing spiritual good to someone so that he or she will be more like Christ. Disciple*ship* is the term I use to describe our own following Christ. Discipl*ing* is the subset of that, which is helping someone else follow Christ.

The Christian life is the discipled life and the discipling life. Yes, Christianity involves taking the road less traveled and hearing a different drummer. But not in the way that Frost and Thoreau meant. Christianity is not for loners or individualists. It is for a people traveling together down the narrow path that leads to life. You must follow and you must lead. You must be loved and you must love. And we love others best by helping them to follow Jesus down the pathway of life.

Is this how you've understood Christianity, and what it means to be a Christian?

WHAT IS A DISCIPLE?

Before we can disciple others, we must become disciples. We must make sure we are following Christ.

What is a disciple? A disciple is a follower. You can do that by following someone's teaching from afar, like someone might say he follows the teaching and example of Gandhi. And being a disciple of Christ means at least that much. A disciple of Jesus follows in Jesus's steps, doing as Jesus taught and lived. But it means more than that. Following Jesus first means that you have entered into a personal, saving relationship with him. You have been "united with Christ," as the Bible puts it (Phil. 2:1, NIV). You have been united through the new covenant in his blood. Through his death and resurrection, all the guilt of sin that is yours becomes his, and all the righteousness that is his becomes yours.

Being a disciple of Christ, in other words, does not begin with something we *do*. It begins with something Christ *did*. Jesus is the Good Shepherd who laid down his life for the sheep (John 10:11). He loved the church and therefore gave himself up for her (Eph. 5:25). He paid a debt that he didn't owe, but that we owe, and then he united us to himself as his holy people.

You see, God is good, and he created us as good. But each of us has sinned by turning away from God and his good law. And because God is good, he will punish our sin. The good news of Christianity, however, is that Jesus lived the perfect life we should have lived, and then he died the death we should die. He offered himself as a substitute and sacrifice for everyone who will repent of their sin and trust in him alone. This is what Jesus called the new covenant in his blood.

So Christian discipleship begins right here with the acceptance of this free gift: grace, mercy, a relationship with God, and the promise of life eternal.

How do we accept this gift and unite ourselves to him? Through faith! We turn away from our sins and follow after him, trusting him as Savior and Lord. At one point in his ministry, Jesus turned toward a crowd and said, "If anyone would come after me, let him deny himself and take up his cross and follow me" (Mark 8:34).

Our discipleship to Christ begins when we hear those two words and obey them: "Follow me."

Friend, if you would become a Christian, regardless of how any other teacher you have heard puts it, listen to Jesus. He says that being a Christian involves denying yourself, taking up your cross, and following him. The fundamental response to God's radical love for us is for us to radically love him.

To be a Christian means to be a disciple. There are no Christians who are not disciples. And to be a disciple of Jesus means to follow Jesus. There are no disciples of Jesus who are not following Jesus. Ticking a box on a public opinion poll, or sincerely labeling yourself with the religion of your parents, or having a preference for Christianity as opposed to other religions—none of these things make you a Christian. Christians are people who have real faith in Christ, and who show it by resting their hopes, fears, and lives entirely upon him. They follow him wherever he leads. You no longer set the agenda for your own life; Jesus Christ does that. You belong to him now. "You are not your own," Paul says, "You were bought with a price" (see 1 Cor. 6:19–20). Jesus is not just our Savior—he is our Lord.

Paul explained it this way: "And he died for all, that those who live should no longer live for themselves but for him who died for them and was raised again" (2 Cor. 5:15 NIV). What does it mean to die to self and live for him? Don Carson has said, "To die to self means to consider it better to die than to lust; to consider it better to die, than to tell this falsehood; than to consider it better to die than to . . . [you name the sin]."

The Christian life is the discipled life. It starts by becoming a disciple of Christ.

WHY DISCIPLE?

But the Christian life is also the discipling life. Disciples disciple. We follow the one who calls people to follow by calling people to follow. Why do we do this? For the sake of love and obedience.

Love. The motive for discipling others begins in the love of God and nothing less. He has loved us in Christ, and so we love him. And we do this in part by loving those he has placed around us.

When a lawyer asks Jesus what the greatest commandment is, Jesus begins by answering, "And you shall love the Lord your God with all your heart and with all your soul and with all your mind and with all your strength" (Mark 12:30). What God wants most of all is for all of you to love him—all your ambitions and motives, your desires and hopes, your thinking and reasoning, your strength and your energy, all of this informed and purified and disciplined by his Word.

In fact, the comprehensiveness of your devotion to God will be demonstrated by your love for those made in God's image. The lawyer may have asked for one command, but he got two: "The second," said Jesus, "is this: 'You shall love your neighbor as yourself.' There is no other commandment greater than these" (v. 31). To omit the second command is to miss the first. Love for God is fundamental to love for neighbor. And love for God must express itself in love for neighbor. It completes the duty of love.

God's love for us starts a chain reaction. He loves us, then we love him, then we love others. John captures all this: "We love because he first loved us. If anyone says, 'I love God,' and hates his brother, he is a liar; for he who does not love his brother whom he has seen cannot love God whom he has not seen. And this commandment we have from him: whoever loves God must also love his brother" (1 John 4:19–21).

Any claim to love for God that does not show itself in a love for neighbor is a love of a false god, another form of idolatry. In these verses Jesus and John reconnect some of the links broken at the fall.

Discipling others—doing deliberate spiritual good to help them follow Christ—demonstrates this love for God and others as well as anything.

Obedience. But tied to our love is our obedience. Jesus taught, "If you love me, you will keep my commandments" (John 14:15; see also 14:23; 15:12–14). And what has he commanded? "Go therefore and make disciples of all nations, baptizing them in the name of the Father and of the Son and of the Holy Spirit, teaching them to observe all that I have commanded you. And behold, I am with you always, to the end of the age" (Matt. 28:19–20). Part of our obedience is leading others to obedience.

Jesus's final command was not to urge his disciples to armed resistance to Rome, or seek revenge on those who killed him. Rather, Jesus looked at his followers, and told them to make disciples, not just be disciples.

Jesus makes no distinction between those to whom this commission was given, and those to whom it wasn't given. He promises his presence to all Christians, as Pentecost would soon show. And that promise extends to the end of the ages, long beyond the apostles' lives. Throughout the rest of the New Testament, all Christians would undertake this work according to their abilities, opportunities, and callings. This Great Commission is given to all those who would be disciples of Jesus. This command is given to every believer at all times.

Discipling is basic to Christianity. How much clearer could it be? We might not be his disciples if we are not laboring to make disciples.

DISCIPLE WHERE AND HOW?

Yet there is one more thing to notice about this final commandment of Jesus. It's where and how he would have us disciple. We are to make disciples among all nations through our churches.

Among all nations. Before telling his disciples to make disciples, he tells them he has received all authority in heaven and earth, and that they should "Go." Jesus's authority is universal, and so is his concern. And the universality of his authority and concern lead to the universality of our mission: we go to all nations. Disciple-making is not just the preserve of Israel or the Middle East or of Africa. Christianity is not only for Europe or Asia. Christ has all authority, and so we go to make disciples of all nations.

Through our churches. After telling the disciples to make disciples, he tells them how—through baptizing and teaching.

Yes, the individual missionary or evangelist goes out into the world, into the office, into the school, into the neighborhood, whether on this side of the globe or the other. But the ministry of the ordinances and the ministry of teaching primarily occur through churches. Churches fulfill the Great Commission, and discipling is the work of churches.

Good fellowship and discipling can occur outside of the context of church membership, to be sure. But through the church's ministry of baptism and the Lord's Supper we recognize one another as believers. And that lends a spiritually beneficial accountability to the discipling relationships. Through the church's and the elders' ministry of teaching, Christians learn to obey everything that Jesus commanded.

The first place Christians should ordinarily look to be discipled and to disciple is through the fellowship of the local church both gathered and scattered. David Wells has observed, "It is very easy to build churches in which seekers congregate; it is very hard to build churches in which biblical faith is maturing into genuine discipleship."[4]

CONCLUSION

The goal of this book is help you understand biblical discipling and to encourage you in your obedience to Christ. Biblical discipling, as I said, is helping others to follow Jesus by doing deliberate spiritual good to them. And biblical discipling largely occurs in and through churches. It's easy for Christians today to miss this.

So when you attend church on Sundays, do you only look for what you can get, or do you also look for ways to give? And how do you use your meals and spare time throughout the week? Do you strategize for evangelism or for ways to build up other Christians?

Maybe you've thought that you really need to be discipled before you can disciple. It is certainly crucial to be a disciple. But Jesus gave the command to make disciples to you. And part of being a disciple, in fact, is to disciple. Part of growing in maturity is helping others grow in maturity. God wants you to be in churches not merely so that your needs are met, but so that you will be equipped and encouraged to care for others.

Christianity—the religion of the Bible—is not for the rugged individual, the self-made man who needs no one else. It's a religion for disciples of Christ, followers who lead others to do the same.

Part 1

WHAT IS DISCIPLING?

1

THE INEVITABILITY
OF INFLUENCE

God's characteristics or "attributes" tell us what God is like. And theologians divide his attributes into two categories: communicable and incommunicable. Communicable attributes may be communicated, or shared, with us. Think of God's love or holiness. We, too, can be loving and holy. His incommunicable attributes, however, are those qualities that only he possesses. Think of his omnipresence (he is everywhere) or omniscience (he knows everything).

One of God's incommunicable attributes is that he is immutable. He doesn't change. We change. He does not.

WE ARE CHANGEABLE CREATURES

Perhaps you are thinking, "You don't know what a creature of habit my husband is!" It's true. I don't. Yet I promise you that, however deep the ruts of habit are in your husband's life, we humans are always changing.

We are born, we grow, we age, we die. All this is change. We learn things we didn't know, and we forget things we did know. We become more godly, or less. All this, too, is change.

And of course circumstances affect us—sometimes for good, other times for ill.

God doesn't change; we do. We are by nature changeable and changing creatures.

Added to that, we live in a world marked by serious spiritual conflict. Peter knew the world pressed in on his readers: "They are surprised when you do not join them in the same flood of debauchery, and they malign you" (1 Pet. 4:4). Paul observed that the ruler of the kingdom of the air "is now at work" in the disobedient (Eph. 2:2). That's why he exhorts us not to be conformed to the pattern of this world, but to be transformed by the renewing of our minds (Rom. 12:2).

Augustine, the fifth-century African pastor, described this spiritual conflict as a clash between two cities, the City of Man and the City of God. And both cities want to recruit us for their work. The underlying reality here is, humans can be changed—positively and negatively.

WE INFLUENCE AND ARE INFLUENCED

Another way to say this is, we human beings are open to being influenced.

Just the other day I walked down to my bank—the same bank that my friend Matt introduced me to when I moved to my neighborhood twenty years ago. Then I walked from there over to the place that cuts my hair—the same place that Matt introduced me to when I moved to my neighborhood twenty years ago. Matt showed me what he did, and so I started doing that. Matt *discipled* me in how to live in our neighborhood. Here I am twenty years later able to find my own way to the bank and the place where you get a haircut. Remember what Jesus said: when a disciple is fully trained, he will be like his teacher (Luke 6:40).

In fact, I want to take this one step further: all of us inevitably will be influenced by others, and we will in turn influence others. "Bad company ruins good morals," says Paul (1 Cor. 15:33), and "a little leaven leavens the whole lump" (5:6). The people around you *will* influence you, for better or worse. And for better or worse you in turn *will* affect the people around you. An absentee father influences his children even in his absence. None of us is an island.

HOW WILL YOU USE YOUR INFLUENCE?

The only question that remains for you is, how will you use your influence?

Maybe you didn't think of yourself as having influence, but you do! You are created in God's own image, and God is so weighty that even the impress of his image bears weight. Your life impacts the people around you, even if you're at the bottom of the totem pole, or you don't feel respected by the people around you.

Consider how Peter instructs the servants of unjust masters or the wives of unbelieving husbands (1 Pet. 2:18–20; 3:1). He knows that both possess influence by their faithfulness. Wives of non-Christian husbands, Peter says, can win those husbands "without a word by the conduct" of their lives. And the example for each is Jesus Christ. Through his suffering, he brought healing and life (2:21–25).

In other words, you will have influence through the gifts

that God has given you in creation. But more than that, you can have gospel influence, and amazingly, making a gospel impact in people's lives doesn't come only through your strengths, but also through your weakness. God does this so that his power would be displayed through our weakness and he would receive all the glory (see 2 Cor. 12:9).

So, again, you *have* influence. How will you use yours? When you step out of the hallway of this life into the room of eternity, what will you have left behind in the lives of others?

According to the Bible, a disciple of Christ disciples others by helping them to follow Christ. Is that how you are exercising your influence?

2

ORIENTED TOWARD OTHERS

If you have never seen pigs come to a trough for mealtime, you can probably imagine it. Pushing. Shoving. Snorting. Swallowing as much as they can with no thought for others.

Here's a funny question worth thinking about for a moment: Is that how you attended church last Sunday?

No, I'm not calling you a pig. But stop and consider: Where did you park? What time did you get to church? Where did you sit? Who did you speak to? Each one of these decisions provided you with an opportunity to give yourself to others and so join in the work of Christ. Or they provided you with an opportunity to look out for yourself, and do what is best for you. So which was it? Did you consciously strategize how to bless others with each one of those decisions?

Being a disciple of Jesus means orienting our lives toward others, just as Jesus did. It means laboring for the sake of others. This love for others is at the heart of discipling. We set our sights on serving others for Christ's sake, just as Christ came into the world not to be served, but to serve and give his life as a ransom for many (Mark 10:45).

The discipling life is an others-oriented life. It labors in the power of God to proclaim Christ and present others mature in Christ. That is the pattern we see in the Bible.

THE BIBLICAL PATTERN

Before Christ is ever named in Scripture, God hardwires these lessons into creation itself through the family. Consider how God makes us parents. He embeds in our nature the desire to give huge amounts of loving attention to rearing one person, nurturing and leading him or her toward maturity.

Then, in ancient Israel, he uses the power of these parenting relationships to work like channels through which the water of his Word flows. So Moses gives the Ten Commandments. He tells the people to love God. And then he instructs the people of Israel, "And these words that I command you today shall be on your heart. You shall teach them diligently to your children, and shall talk of them when you sit in your house, and when you walk by the way, and when you lie down, and when you rise" (Deut. 6:6–7). Here God gives us a great object lesson in discipling another human being. Discipling involves transmitting the knowledge of God and his Word through every moment of life.

Beyond the family itself, the Bible is full of discipling relationships where one person teaches another. Think of how Moses raised up Joshua to succeed him. As did Eli with Samuel. And Elijah with Elisha.

The most famous discipler of all, of course, is Jesus Christ. Christianity did not start with a mass-market product rollout. There was no 24/7 media coverage surrounding his travels. It began with a series of personal engagements among a small group of men over a three-year period.

Yes, crowds often came to Jesus, and word of his miracles sometimes spread like wildfire. But within those large crowds was a smaller group of disciples whom Jesus called to himself. He invested particularly in them. Mark's Gospel tells us that Jesus "called to him those whom he desired, and they came to him. And he appointed twelve (whom he also named apostles) so that they might be with him and he might send them out to preach" (Mark 3:13–14).

These Twelve confessed that Jesus is the Messiah. They largely stayed with him. And he wanted them to "be with him." (I love that phrase!) Within the Twelve, he especially poured into three: Peter, James, and John.

But you might say, "That's Jesus! Of course he does this. He's God!"

All right then. Let's consider the example of the apostle Paul. Acts 16 describes one of Paul's missionary journeys. But the chapter begins by introducing us to a disciple named Timothy and then tells us, "Paul wanted Timothy to accompany him" (v. 3). Like Jesus and the disciples, Paul wanted Timothy to be with him, to travel with him, to join him in the work of the kingdom. It's not difficult to surmise that Paul discipled Timothy like an Old Testament father would disciple his son— teaching God's Word diligently when they walked by the way, when they lay down, when they rose.

Decades later, Paul would tell Timothy to do the same with others: "What you have heard from me in the presence of many witnesses entrust to faithful men who will be able to teach others also" (2 Tim. 2:2). Paul's discipling ambitions were multigenerational. He wanted spiritual great-grandchildren. Timothy (child) was to find faithful men (grandchildren) who would be able to teach others (great-grandchildren).

TOILING AND STRUGGLING

What would it mean to give yourself to this biblical pattern of investing in spiritual children? This whole book will address that question. But Colossians 1:28–29 provides a useful starting point.

When I was a young Christian, I chose these two verses as my "life verses." In them, Paul is writing to the church at Colossae, a city in what is today western Turkey. He reminds these Christians of what he has done for them: "Him we proclaim, warning everyone and teaching everyone with all wisdom, that we may present everyone mature in Christ. For this I toil, struggling with all his energy that he powerfully works within me" (Col. 1:28–29).

Paul toils. Paul struggles. If we would do good for others, so must we.

Do you ever wonder how to exercise spiritual power? Maybe people will tell you, "Eat this." "Say these words." "Pray this prayer." "Read this author." "Have this experience." "Go to this conference." "Look inside yourself."

But no! Spiritual power is exercised in strenuous self-giving service for others. The word for *struggling* in Colossians 1:29 can also be translated as "agony." Which is to say, agony rather than ecstasy is the way to spiritual power. Do you want to know the power of God and a faith that works? Then give yourself over to the struggle of working for the good of others, even as Christ himself worked and struggled for our good.

True Christian faith is not lazy faith. It is faith that works, like Paul's.

GOD'S POWERFUL WORK

But is Paul bragging by talking about his toil and struggle on their behalf? Not at all. Look at the last words in the passage: *God* was powerfully working within him. Whatever the Colossians had received from Paul, it wasn't to Paul's credit, it was to God's.

If you or I hope to contribute any good to others, if we hope to influence others for Christ's sake, as we talked about in the last chapter, it will only happen as God's Spirit works in us and through us.

Knowing that God works in us counters pride. It reminds us that all that we have and are, all that we can do and achieve, comes from God. If you or I have observed any fruitfulness from our labors, there's no reason for pride. God has worked. It was his power. All spiritual fruit redounds to his praise.

And knowing that God works counters fear. If we are certain of God's good work in us, if we are committed to his goals, we can lay aside the fear that our work is futile or misdirected. We can lay aside the fear of losing health or wealth. Such things may go, but his work through us will last eternally.

PROCLAIM AND PRESENT

Notice the two words in these same verses that tell us what Paul means to do—proclaim and present: "Him we *proclaim* . . .

that we may *present* everyone mature in Christ." He proclaims so that he can present. Proclaim the Word of God now; present the saints mature in Christ when he comes later. These two words tell us how Paul toils and struggles (by proclaiming), as well as why he toils and struggles (so that he might present).

Paul also explains what's involved in proclaiming: "Him we proclaim, warning everyone and teaching everyone with all wisdom." Paul's proclaiming involves warning and teaching. He warns churches away from what's worthless and damning and teaches them to be united in the riches and wisdom of the gospel. And he doesn't just warn and teach all people abstractly. He warns *everyone* and teaches *everyone*—from person to person to person.

A few verses later Paul describes his desire for the Colossians to possess "the full riches of complete understanding" (2:2 NIV). Notice the piled-up goods: *full riches* of *complete* understanding! There are treasures of wisdom and knowledge to be found here! Part of maturity is knowing how to discern between right and wrong, true and false, precious and worthless. This is how Paul wants to present God's people fully mature, fully grown.

The work of discipling occurs in the present, but it has its eyes set on the Last Day. It requires long-term thinking. It requires an investor's mentality, knowing that the return is eternal. And the investment occurs through God's Word. We must proclaim. God's Word is the seed that ultimately bears fruit, even if we don't see it in the short term. Sow the Word now. Sow with your spouse and children. Sow with other members of the church. And trust that God's Word does not return void. You will see the harvest later. Mature believers will be ready to receive Christ when he comes.

Living for others typifies Paul's whole life. He even writes letters to Christians he has not met, like this one to the Colossians to encourage them in the gospel. We could say that his life was cruciform—formed in the pattern of the cross. He heeded Christ's call to take up Christ's cross and follow him. Like Christ, he suffered in obedience to God for the good of others.

Is that you? Imagine what it might be like to work with "all God's energy powerfully working" in you!

A BRIEF WORD TO PASTORS

If you are a pastor or are considering the pastoral ministry, you should think long and hard about this passage. Notice that the ministry involves both fully proclaiming the Word of God and working to present the people of God mature before him.

This requires utter selflessness on our part. There is much that is good about being a pastor, but, given the sinfulness in both church members and pastors, there is also much that's tough. Pastor, you will toil and struggle out of love for the members of your congregation, and they sometimes will respond by explaining how flawed and insufficient your love is.

Ultimately, therefore, your toil and labor cannot root in your love for them or their love for you. It must root in your love for Christ, his love for you, and his love for them. He has purchased them with his blood. And you mean to present them *to him*. It is *for him* that you do it all.

Of course, this word applies to all Christians. We disciple

and teach and warn so that we can present the people we love to God, because we most love him, because he most loved us.

TRUE FAITH WORKS FOR OTHERS

True Christian faith is not pig-like. It does not look out only for itself, and it is not lazy. Like Paul, it works. It works for others. It works with the energy supplied by God who works powerfully in us. It works by proclaiming, warning, and teaching. And it works so that others might be presented mature in Christ on the day of his coming.

We don't always see immediate fruit. To disciple, you must be like the patient farmer who plants his crops, trusting that they will eventually spring up. We trust God to use his Word, even if we never see the fruit. As one writer said, "The seed may lie under the clods until we lie there, and *then spring up!*"[1]

For me, discipling is the only way I can evangelize non-Christians and equip Christians in that one place where I can never travel—the future beyond my life. Discipling others now is how I try to leave time-bombs of grace.

A disciple is one who disciples. He proclaims now so that he might present later. So name a couple of people in your life whom you would love to see presented mature and godly on the Last Day. Got their names in mind? Now, how are you proclaiming the gospel to them now to prepare them for then?

3

THE WORK OF DISCIPLING

Discipling does not seem like the most obvious way to establish and strengthen a kingdom. Kingdom building is typically the stuff of royal battles, dynastic wars, great fortunes, or works of political philosophy by old men with long gray beards.

But Jesus concluded his time on earth commanding his disciples to make disciples. Is that really how his kingdom would be built? In fact, recall what Jesus had taught earlier:

> The kingdom of heaven is like a grain of mustard seed that a man took and sowed in his field. It is the smallest of all seeds, but when it has grown it is larger than all the garden plants and becomes a tree, so that the birds of the air come and make nests in its branches. (Matt. 13:31–32)

Jesus taught his disciples to live in view not of today or tomorrow, but eternity. We try to help others follow Jesus; we do deliberate spiritual good; we pray for gospel influence; we proclaim God's words, and we do all this for the sake of the Last Day. Yes, we may see some fruit now. But the goal is always to present people mature in Christ then.

Can we say anything further about what discipling is? I've said it's helping others follow Jesus. It's doing them spiritual good. But to fill all that out, discipling is initiating a relationship in which you teach, correct, model, and love. It takes great humility.

INITIATING

Discipling necessarily involves initiating. It's not passive. And that can feel awkward. You cannot disciple everybody, so you have to pick this person and not that one. Practically, do your schedules overlap?

You also have to discern not just who needs help, but who knows they need help and is willing to receive it. In general, you don't want to waste time with people who are not teachable, because you *will be* wasting time. Look instead for people who, like the wise son in Proverbs, welcome counsel and instruction.

Keep in mind, discipling among gospel-believers doesn't mean you as the discipler always play the wise one, or that you must be a fount of Socrates-like wisdom with all the answers. Discipling in the gospel means that sometimes you lead the way in confessing weakness or sin. By doing so, you demonstrate what it looks like not to find your justification in yourself, but in Christ. And so you live transparently and honestly. Christian discipleship, in other words, isn't just about displaying your strengths; it's about displaying your weakness, too. "But we have this treasure in jars of clay to show that this all-surpassing power is from God and not from us" (2 Cor. 4:7 NIV).

Still, you initiate in relationship, even if it's they who have asked you to disciple them. You are the one who, to some measure, leads the relationship by deliberately using your time together to point toward the way of Christ. The wife of the non-Christian husband, whom we thought about in chapter 1, does this if nothing else by her faithful actions.

OUTSIDE THE CHURCH, INSIDE THE CHURCH

The first stage of discipling can involve establishing a friendship with a non-Christian. You explain the gospel and call him to repentance and faith. Once he repents and believes, he should be baptized into church membership. Discipling in the fullest sense, in other words, includes evangelism and conversion.

At the same time, if your church is like mine, it regularly receives the gift of new members who are already converted, yet are young in the faith. The Great Commission's command to make disciples through the ministry of the ordinances and teaching obliges us to disciple them, both individually and corporately. Together we sit under the preached Word, and together we enjoy the Lord's Supper to proclaim the Lord's death and to remind one another that "we who are many are one body" (1 Cor. 10:17).

When the church scatters, the ministry of teaching and oversight should continue in the lives of members. This happens over weeknight desserts or Saturday morning breakfasts, while folding laundry or taking trips to the grocery store. Discipling lasts all week as members meet to talk, pray, encourage, and assist one another in the fight for love and holiness.

TEACHING

At its core, discipling is teaching. We teach with words. We teach all the words that Jesus taught his disciples, and all the words of the Bible.

Corporately, this is why my own church preaches expositionally and consecutively through books of the Bible, alternating between the Old and New Testaments, as well as between big chunks of Scripture and little ones. We also encourage people to attend our adult Sunday school program that provides a several-year curriculum through different areas of the Christian life. Once people complete the curriculum, we encourage them to walk someone else through the curriculum. Our church also finds lots of ways to promote the ministry of good books.

Interpersonally, teaching occurs as people learn to have spiritually meaningful conversations with each other, which is something that I as the pastor encourage from the front almost every week. It's fine to talk about football or the kids' school. But talk about Sunday's sermon, as well. Ask your friends what God has been teaching you about himself. Small groups can also be useful for facilitating these kinds of relationships.

CORRECTING

Sometimes discipling requires you to warn someone about the choices he or she is making. People grow when you teach them general truths, yes, but also when you correct their particular errors. Part of being a Christian is recognizing that sin deceives us, and we need other believers to help us see the things we cannot see about ourselves. Joining a church, I've often said, is like throwing paint on the invisible man. New sins become visible in the course of our discipling relationships.

In fact, you can lead in a discipling relationship by inviting others to correct you, and making it easy for them to do so. But you must fear God more than man by being willing to correct others when necessary, and risk their rejection of you for it.

Ultimately, the work of correction belongs to the whole congregation, which occurs when a member proves more committed to his or her sin than to Christ. After multiple rounds of warning, the person will be excluded from membership and the Lord's Table (Matt. 18:15–20). The vast majority of correction in a church, however, should occur in the private context of discipling relationships.

MODELING

It's worth noticing that Jesus didn't just command his disciples *to teach people*. He told them *to teach people to obey*. The goal of discipling is to see lives transformed, which means it involves more than reading a book or even the Bible with another person. Ultimately, discipling involves living out the whole Christian life before others. Christ is our example here. He "left you an example that you should follow" (1 Pet. 2:21).

We communicate not merely with our words but by our whole lives. And what happens in a discipling relationship requires more than classroom teaching (like we do every Sunday). It requires the kind of instruction that occurs through an apprenticeship at a job, or with a personal trainer or coach. An apprentice learns by listening *and* watching *and* participating, little by little, with more responsibility being earned over time. Most of all, discipling looks like what God designed for the home, where dads and moms teach in word and deed through all areas of life, and then draw the children into the work of adulthood.

Really, discipling is a kind of fashion modeling. No, you're not showing off clothes for a photographer; you're demonstrating a fashion, or way of living, for others to follow. Discipling is inviting them to imitate you, making your trust in Christ an example to be followed. It requires you to be willing to be watched, and then folding people into your life so that they actually do watch. Each one of the elders in my church, for instance, does exactly this, so that our members can heed the counsel of Hebrews: "Remember your leaders, those who spoke to you the word of God. Consider the outcome of their way of life, and imitate their faith" (13:7). All of us, in turn, should be able to say to the other Christians in our lives, as Paul did, "Be imitators of me, as I am of Christ" (1 Cor. 11:1). Maybe this is why Christian biographies are so useful.

MUTUAL LOVE

To add another angle, discipling is a form of mutual love. There is something of a teacher-student relationship. But there will also be peer-to-peer mutuality and love, such that the discipling often goes both ways. As one who has been doing this for a long time, I can say that I've often been served and blessed and encouraged in the faith by those whom I am discipling. Even as I work to do them spiritual good, they do me spiritual good. They help me better follow Jesus. Together we learn what

Paul means in Colossians 3:16: "Let the word of Christ dwell in you richly, teaching and admonishing one another in all wisdom. . . ."

Together we work to fulfill Hebrews 10:24–25: "Let us consider how we may spur one another on toward love and good works, not neglecting to meet together, as is the habit of some, but encouraging one another, and all the more as you see the Day drawing near." In discipling, my goal is to love younger Christians by helping them live in light of the Final Day, but they typically recognize that my ability to do this depends on them helping me to do the same.

HUMILITY

There's more I'll say in later chapters about how to do all this. But let me observe for the time being that helping others follow Jesus cannot be done without risk. Just as you have to humble yourself to be discipled, so you have to humble yourself to disciple. Discipling involves difficult things—saying no, persevering through troubles, knowing when to bear with someone, and *doing* it. Your invitations might be spurned, your counsel rejected.

As noted earlier, we disciple not just through our strength, but through our weakness. Christian discipling is not so much the work of experts and technocrats; to borrow the old phrase, it's the work of one beggar pointing another beggar to bread.

Erin Wheeler, wife to Brad who pastored with me in Washington, DC, before taking a church elsewhere, reflected in a 9Marks article how she had to learn these lessons during their time in DC. Another woman in the church showed up at Erin's house expecting to be discipled. Erin welcomed her inside, closed the door behind her, and thought to herself,

> I am a mess. I have no idea what I'm doing here. There certainly isn't any "teaching" going on today with my crazy hooligan children and my heart in a bad place toward my husband. I shouldn't be teaching anyone. I'm the one who needs discipling! God, what would you have me do?

Yet God would soon teach Erin through situations like these that he would use her weakness as much as her strength. These younger women in the faith needed someone to teach them what it looks like to love God with heart, soul, mind, and strength not just in the good times, but in the challenging times. Erin explains,

> In discipling these women I tried to instruct and question them, discuss books together, and pray, but they would tell me later that often the best teaching came from simply watching me. They watched God use my weakness in fighting for patience when the day had long since worn me thin. They watched me struggle to love my husband after sharing my struggles with the competing demands of ministry.

These women got a front-row seat, she observes, to seeing the true jar of clay that she is (2 Cor. 4:7). But learning this gospel perspective encouraged her to keep pouring herself out like a drink offering (Phil. 2:17), knowing that God would use her frailty as a platform to display his strength. And sure enough: again and again God proved faithful to supply everything she needed to love and serve these younger sisters. She concludes:

Years later, God brought a new friend and sister into the church who would come over to hang out on any Saturday afternoon that my husband was busy preparing a sermon. Every time she came over it seemed like something was going wrong, from a fit of rage in one of my children to the toilet overflowing! It was during one of those times that I looked up at her with a smile, confident in the Lord's perfect timing, and said, "You know, God must really love you to let you see all this."

That is our confidence: not that we have the perfect home and well-behaved children, but that in the muck and mire, God's Spirit is at work. Even in our weakness, God uses our words to warn those who are idle, encourage the timid, comfort the weak, and show patience to everyone, all for his great glory. [1]

The local church is the best place for such relationships to grow, as I will observe shortly. A church can be thick with mentoring relationships even if they are not formally called "discipling relationships." After all, discipling really is just a bunch of church members taking responsibility to prepare one another for glory, as Erin and these women did for each other. It's one way we see the New Testament idea that we are a kingdom of priests and a holy nation (1 Pet. 2:9). How much *pastoring* gets done in the ordinary life of a congregation when it's characterized by a culture of discipling!

One last place humility is required comes with the recognition that people will sometimes move away. The reality of transience, particularly in many cities, requires us to maintain open-handedness toward these people we love. We don't invest and share and pour in and pray and love for what we might receive—other than the satisfaction and joy that comes from knowing they are better equipped for wherever they go next, and ultimately for Christ's coming.

GUIDING TOWARD HEAVEN

To be human is to be a disciple. God didn't present Adam and Eve with a choice between discipleship and independence, but between following him and following Satan. We are all disciples; the only question is, of whom? Are we following other believers toward the heavenly city, and helping still more to do the same?

I love how Charles Spurgeon describes his own ministry. In his autobiography, he compares himself to Mr. Great-heart, the character in John Bunyan's *The Pilgrim's Progress* who helps others toward the Celestial City.

> I am occupied in my small way, as Mr. Great-heart was employed in Bunyan's day. I do not compare myself with that champion, but I am in the same line of business. I am engaged in personally-conducted tours to Heaven. . . . It is my business, as best I can, to kill dragons, and cut off giants' heads, and lead on the timid and trembling. I am often afraid of losing some of the weaklings. I have the heart-ache for them; but, by God's grace, and your kind and generous help in looking after one another, I hope we shall all travel safely to the river's edge. Oh, how many have I had to part with there! I have stood on the brink, and I have heard them singing in the midst of the stream, and I have almost seen the shining ones lead them up the hill, and through the gates, into the Celestial City.[2]

4

OBJECTIONS TO DISCIPLING

I realize that I've been using the word *discipling* where others use different words. In Britain, the phrase *reading with* seems more common. Here in the States, people refer to having an accountability partner or prayer partner. Whatever you call it, I am using the word as shorthand for helping others follow Jesus by doing deliberate spiritual good in their lives. It involves taking initiative, teaching, modeling, love, and humility.

But even if we can agree on the term, some Christians still have a difficult time with the whole concept of discipling. They feel awkward. They don't want to impose unwanted ideas on others. They don't want to act as if they were "above" other people.[1]

An infinite number of objections can be raised. But let me share with you a few, along with my quick responses.

Objection 1: "This discipler is not ideal."
Answer: Neither are you. God's the only perfect one in this equation. He gets glory by using imperfect vessels like me and

like you. The more humble you are, the more you'll find you have to learn from any other true disciple.

Objection 2: "If a person is always listening to her discipler, she might no longer submit to other good authorities like parents, husband, or church."

Answer: Done well, good discipling will encourage appropriate submission to any authorities established by God.

Objection 3: "This whole things seems self-centered and prideful."

Answer: I understand how it could seem like that. But Christian discipling calls us to follow someone *only* insofar as he or she follows Christ. It doesn't call us to follow another's style, or cultural preferences, or worldly wisdom, or personal habits. Insofar as the practice of discipling calls us to model and imitate Christ for one another, it's really very humbling. Beyond all this, it's simply biblical.

Objection 4: "Isn't it just pushy, and aren't you imposing yourself on someone else?"

Answer: Christian discipling works through a mutually agreed upon relationship.

Objection 5: I don't need it. I mean, surely the most important things about the Christian life are self-evident! So I'm too busy for this to be a priority.

Answer: This sounds like the "Lone Ranger" syndrome. Jesus died not for separate individuals, but for a church. By adopting you, God brought you into a family, so that now you have brothers and sisters. What's more, he says we demonstrate our family membership and love for him through our love for one another. We do that through our submission to and fellowship with a local church. Christianity is personal, yes, always!—but not private. You need to be involved in the lives of others, and you need them in yours. God is the only one who doesn't need to be taught!

Objection 6: "This is just for extroverts."
Answer: No, this is for Christians. The number of these relationships you might have will vary according to personality, life circumstances, and so forth. But having none of them is not an option for a faith centered on love and forgiveness. Speak to other mature Christians to help you sort through this in your own life.

Objection 7: "I can't disciple. I'm imperfect, erring, and too young!"
Answer: If you are truly following Christ, all you need to do is share what you *do* know, not what you don't know. For many people around you, that will mean sharing the gospel! With fellow church members, this may mean initiating spiritual conversations by asking questions, sharing what you're learning, and praying for them. Anyone truly following Christ can disciple.

CONCLUSION

Discipling is helping someone follow Jesus by doing deliberate spiritual good in his or her life. We are Christians because someone did that for us, and someone did it for them, all the way back to the earliest disciples. The original eyewitnesses of Jesus taught what he had commanded them to, and so created *ear*-witnesses. This continues down to the present day, and now it's our turn. Under the sovereignty of God, the future generation of disciples depends on us following the example of these first disciples. Discipling is part of our own discipleship to Christ.

•••

But so far I have mostly been encouraging discipling as a one-on-one activity. And some of our discipling relationships with other believers may occur outside shared membership in a church. Yet in order for the love of Christ to be displayed clearly to the world around us (see John 13:34–35), much of our discipling will occur within the context of the local church. Every Christian needs not just another Christian— each of us needs a whole body! That's what we'll talk about in the next section.

Part 2

WHERE SHOULD WE DISCIPLE?

5

THE LOCAL CHURCH

Dawson Trotman has a remarkable story. In the early 1930s, Trotman, a young lumberyard worker, became inspired by 2 Timothy 2:2: "What you have heard from me in the presence of many witnesses entrust to faithful men who will be able to teach others also." He began teaching high school students to disciple one another, and then, in 1933, extended this work to the United States Navy, founding a group called The Navigators. He mentored one sailor, who in turn mentored many more on board the USS *West Virginia*. Before the ship sank at Pearl Harbor, 125 men were growing in Christ and sharing their faith. During World War II, The Navigators ministry spread to thousands in the United States Navy on ships and bases around the world.

The Navigators continued working in the growing military population until 1951 when it also began to work with college students on the campus of the University of Nebraska. Trotman died in 1956 rescuing a young girl from drowning in upstate New York. But the work went on. Today, hundreds of college campuses around the world have a Navigators group evangelizing and discipling students.

The Navigators website describes the organization as "a

Christian ministry that helps people grow in Jesus Christ as they navigate through life." They also say, "We spread the Good News of Jesus Christ by establishing life-on-life mentoring— or discipling—relationships with people, equipping them to make an impact on those around them for God's glory." I am thankful for their ministry, especially in this area of discipling.

BUT WHAT ABOUT THE CHURCH?

Having said that, it is interesting that these two summary statements describe what churches should be doing!

Some people raise concerns about parachurch ministries like The Navigators replacing the church. *Para* means *beside*, and it's worth asking whether these parachurch ministries really work beside churches or *apart* from them. Certainly there are some circumstances—such as sailors on a battleship in the middle of the Pacific Ocean—that require discipling apart from the local church. It would be tragically wrong, however, to use something like a campus ministry or a businessman's fellowship to replace the local church when it comes to making and growing disciples, as if you were trapped on a ship at sea.

If it's unwise to do discipling without a church, it's worse to do church without discipling. Yet isn't that the case with many local churches?

Christians join churches, and no one comes alongside them. There is no culture of single folks living with families to learn how to serve Christ. No culture of sharing the gospel with international students. Little hospitality. Only occasional invitations to Sunday lunch or Thursday night dinner. No men shepherding their wives, and no wives or older women generally discipling the younger women. No biblical counseling among the members themselves—counseling occurs only in offices. No thought of going to a church where the style of music may not be your favorite, even though it serves others. No thought of helping a family or marriage in trouble. Little reaching out to people with a different skin color or accent. Few if any young men meeting up with other young men to study Scripture.

With churches like this, it's not surprising that some have turned to parachurch ministries. Their experience has taught them that the local church is the last place to look for discipling opportunities.

THE CHURCH ITSELF AS THE DISCIPLER

Yet the Bible teaches that the local church is the natural environment for discipling. In fact, it teaches that the local church *is itself* the basic discipler of Christians. It does this through its weekly gatherings and its accountability structures (this chapter), as well as its elders and its members (next chapter). These in turn provide the context for the one-on-one discipling we have been considering so far.

The gathered local church is responsible to preach the whole counsel of God through those gifted for this purpose. Through baptism it affirms credible professions. Through the Lord's Supper it declares the Lord's death and makes the many into one. And through excommunication it removes anyone whose life unrepentantly contradicts his or her profession.

That much provides a church's skeletal structure. Then we come to the realm of relationships, which are like the church's flesh and muscle. In their life together, the members of a church practice loving one another as Jesus has loved them: "A new commandment I give to you, that you love one another: just as I have loved you, you also are to love one another. By this all people will know that you are my disciples, if you have love for one another" (John 13:34–35). With what kind of love did Jesus love his disciples? He loved them with a love that continually pointed to the words of the Father. That demonstrated his love through obeying the Father. That assured them of a place being prepared for them. That ultimately laid down his life so that they could be forgiven. Now think: Where can we, too, best love like this? Answer: In an environment where we can love by pointing to the words of the Father and Son, by affirming repentance through baptism, by affirming that the many are one through the Supper, and by sacrificing our own agendas and vendettas through forgiveness. Flesh and skeleton come together. In these most basic ways, the local church is the primary discipler of all Christians.

Our churches will never be perfect. But if heaven is what Jonathan Edwards called "a world of love" (and as 1 Corinthians 13 implies), then a local church should be a preview or foretaste of that world.

GATHERING TOGETHER

The church's discipling work begins quite simply by gathering together. The author of Hebrews writes, "And let us consider how to stir up one another to love and good works, not neglecting to meet together, as is the habit of some, but encouraging one another, and all the more as you see the Day drawing near" (10:24–25).

Notice that the goal here is to help one another follow Jesus, or, as Hebrews puts it, stir one another up to love and good works. And how does the author say a church accomplishes that goal? By not neglecting meeting together. By gathering! This is how we "encourage" one another. He means for us to repeatedly and regularly gather, and that regular meeting gives shape to following Jesus and helping others follow Jesus.

AN AUTHORITY STRUCTURE

This was Jesus's own design. Jesus had been discipling the Twelve for some time when he asked them who he was. Peter professed that Jesus was the long-promised Messiah. Jesus affirms Peter's answer on behalf of the "Father who is in heaven," and then he promises to build his church on this rightly professing Peter. Then, interestingly, Jesus begins to put an authority structure in place. He gives Peter the authority to do what Jesus had done with him: to bind and loose "on earth" what's bound and loosed "in heaven." That is to say, Peter and the apostles would be able to hear people's confessions, and then affirm or deny those confessions and confessors on behalf of heaven, like Jesus had done with Peter (Matt. 16:13–20).

Later, Jesus then puts this same authority into the hands of the local church. Envisioning a situation in which a man's profession of faith contradicted his life, Jesus gives the gathered church the authority to bind and loose. The church would need to judge whether to continue affirming someone's profession or to exclude the individual from membership (see Matt. 18:15–20).

In short, the gathered assembly possesses the authority to affirm or disaffirm who belongs to the body of Christ, or who is a disciple. And in so doing it provides the context of accountability for discipling. Is this person I'm discipling an unbeliever? A believer? Someone who needs to be told he is living like an unbeliever?

BAPTIZING AND TEACHING ONE ANOTHER

How exactly does a church affirm who the disciples are? Through baptism and the Lord's Supper. After invoking all authority in heaven and on earth, Jesus commands his disciples to go and "make disciples of all nations, baptizing them in the name of the Father, and of the Son, and of the Holy Spirit, teaching them. . . ." To baptize someone is to formally recognize, "He is with Jesus." These Jesus representatives must then be taught (Matt. 28:18–20). And through the Lord's Supper, Paul says, "We who are many are one body" (1 Cor. 10:17).

Moving into the book of Acts and the Epistles, we find the apostles' discipling program. They're not just freely roving disciplers among unaffiliated groups of people. Rather, they baptize people into churches, where any one-on-one discipling and fellowship would then occur. So Peter preaches the gospel at Pentecost; people repent and get baptized; the people gather regularly both in homes and in the temple courts for the breaking of bread; and all this adds up to a church, the church in Jerusalem. The disciples then spread out to the nations and make disciples *not apart* from baptizing and teaching, or *apart* from the Lord's Supper, or *apart* from teachers gifted by God. No, the disciples plant churches that obey and teach others to obey.

In the New Testament, the local church is at the very center of the disciples' obedience and discipling work. It's not optional; it's basic. We'll think about this further in the next chapter, particularly in terms of the elders' and members' work.

6

PASTORS AND MEMBERS

The local church is the natural arena for discipling relation-ships, as we considered in the last chapter. We thought about discipling in the context of the church's gathering. And we thought about the accountability churches have through the ordinances. Yet there are two more matters worth exploring in the life of the church: the work of the pastors and the re-sponsibility of the congregation or members. These two things are also crucial for the ordinary work of discipling in a Chris-tian's life.

PASTORS DISCIPLE AND EQUIP DISCIPLERS WITH GOD'S WORD

Let's start by thinking about pastors. In the New Testament, the fundamental role of the pastor or elder (the Bible uses the two words interchangeably) is to disciple by teaching God's Word. Initially they do this as evangelists. Paul tells Timothy to "do the work of an evangelist" (2 Tim. 4:5) since faith comes from hearing the word of Christ (Rom. 10:17).

But more broadly, God sets pastors apart to disciple the church by teaching them God's Word. Pastors teach both in corporate gatherings and in one-on-one or small group set-tings. And one of their goals in teaching is to equip the church for works of ministry so that the church can build itself up in love (Eph. 4:11–16). They disciple members so that members can disciple.

What a gift pastors or elders are to the church! Peter is a great example of this. He preached evangelistically at Pentecost. And he wrote letters to the saints. Both teaching and writing, furthermore, were expositions of God's Word from the Old Testament.

Paul is a good example, too. He told the young pastor Timothy to keep a close watch on his teaching (1 Tim. 4:16). And both of his letters to Timothy are shot through with his concern that pastors be men of the Word, shaped by it themselves and able to teach others also.

The best thing I can say about time spent in a church where you're not normally hearing God's Word is that you're wasting your time. That's because pastors teaching the Word is the core of a church's discipling ministry. It provides the food and water that feeds all the other discipling relationships within the church. You experienced it last Sunday, and hopefully you experienced it the last time you sought counsel from an elder. If you didn't, change churches; find a church where God's Word will be taught to you—for your soul's sake and for the sake of you helping others.

PASTORS LEAD IN BAPTISM AND THE LORD'S SUPPER

Tied to the ministry of the Word is the ministry of the ordinances. The ordinances, too, teach. The Supper, for instance, "proclaims" Christ's death until he comes again (1 Cor. 11:26). Insofar as the ordinances "mark off" the church, however, they also provide accountability for the Christian life, as we considered in the last chapter. They designate who the members are.

Leading in these teaching and accountability matters are the pastors. Generally speaking, they do the work of interviewing baptismal candidates and prospective members: "How did you become a Christian?" "What is the gospel?" As a congregationalist, I believe the congregation possesses final authority over decisions of membership and who receives the ordinances. But ordinarily the congregation should follow the leadership of the elders. The elders lead, too, when a matter of discipline reaches the whole congregation. They teach the church what it means to confront unrepentant sin by recommending removing someone from the Lord's Table and membership as an act of excommunication.

In all of these ways, the elders help to give a church its form and make it an environment where discipling can flourish. They make it easier for members to disciple one another. They keep it from being an unaccountable crowd of informal friendships where no one is formally responsible for anyone else, and where each person is left to define the gospel and gospel faithfulness for himself. When there is not accountability, how easy is it for one young believer to disciple another? How does he even know who the believers are as opposed to the heretics or hypocrites?

PASTORS PROVIDE AN EXAMPLE

We have already seen that modeling the way of the cross is a crucial component of discipling generally. Remember that Paul said, "Be imitators of me, as I am of Christ" (1 Cor. 11:1).

The elders are men given by the Spirit and recognized by the congregation as exemplary models. They are not perfect, but they are above reproach. This is why Paul emphasizes the importance of character when describing their qualities to Timothy and Titus (1 Tim. 3:1–7; Titus 1:6–9). The author of Hebrews also counsels, "Remember your leaders, those who spoke to you the word of God. Consider the outcome of their way of life, and imitate their faith" (13:7). Notice he doesn't exhort his readers to follow the example of just any leaders; he tells them to follow "your" leaders.

It's all well and good for you to learn through the books of pastors who are dead and gone. It's fine for you to enjoy the sermons of other preachers on the Internet. But Scripture calls you to imitate the faith of the pastors *who spoke to you* the Word of God. These are the men who will give an account for you (Heb. 13:17). The stakes are higher for them. So watch their lives as part of your discipleship, and from them learn how to disciple others.

The local church is the natural arena for discipling relationships, because that's where the pastors are!

THE CONGREGATION RECEIVES AND SUPPORTS THE PASTORS' MINISTRY

But now let's consider how the congregation helps to make the local church a natural arena for discipling relationships, starting with how they receive and support the elders' ministry. You realize, don't you, that the congregation's reception and support of the elders as gifts from Christ makes their ministry possible? They need the congregation's love and prayers as well as their cheerful support. A church "works" when the members honor and submit to their pastors. Too easily do Christians overlook this dynamic.

Consider how Paul exhorts the Thessalonians: "We ask you, brothers, to respect those who labor among you and are over you in the Lord and admonish you, and to esteem them very highly in love because of their work" (1 Thess. 5:12–13). Those who rule well and teach, he says, are worthy of "double honor" (1 Tim. 5:17), which is a financial term. To the Galatians he says, "Let the one who is taught the word share all good things with the one who teaches" (6:6). If a brother is gifted by God and called to teach his Word, a church will benefit by helping him to arrange his life so that he can concentrate on teaching. His ability to equip them depends upon their receiving him.

THE CONGREGATION MUST SOMETIMES REJECT THE PASTORS' MINISTRY

At the same time, a congregation also helps to foster a culture of discipling by being ready to reject the elders whenever the elders reject God's Word. If discipling means helping others follow Jesus, congregations that tolerate bad teachers are not helping others follow Jesus. Sadly, too many pastors have rejected God's Word, and too many churches have not recognized their responsibility in this matter. The New Testament teaches that a congregation will share responsibility for the serious false teaching that it endures. Paul blames not just false teachers, but the members who have itching ears and accumulate for themselves teachers to suit their own passions (2 Tim. 4:3).

The Bible recognizes the responsibility of the congregation to reject false teachers. Paul even tells the churches in Galatia they can pull rank on him if he departs from the gospel: "But even if we or an angel from heaven should preach to you a gospel contrary to the one we preached to you, let him be accursed" (Gal. 1:8). I therefore regularly tell my church to "fire me" if I compromise Scripture.

Knowing that you as a church member possess this responsibility should increase your sense of the seriousness of membership. It requires you to know the gospel, study the gospel, and generally give careful attention to God's Word! In short, it makes you a better discipler.

MEMBERS ARE RESPONSIBLE FOR ONE ANOTHER

The members of a church are also responsible for one another. The whole congregation is responsible to make sure that each member—Sarah and Stephanie, Nick and Joe—are loved and spurred on to love (e.g., 1 Cor. 12:12–26; Heb. 10:24). We are one body: "For the body does not consist of one member but of many. If the foot should say, 'Because I am not a hand, I do not belong to the body,' that would not make it any less a part of the body" (1 Cor. 12:14–15).

This responsibility takes a lot of forms. Just count up the "one anothers" in one short passage from Paul: "Love one another with brotherly affection. Outdo one another in showing honor. . . . Contribute to the needs of the saints and seek to show hospitality. . . . Rejoice with those who rejoice, weep with those who weep. Live in harmony with one another" (Rom.

12:10–16). This is a community that takes responsibility for its own members.

Yet what I want you to see here is that these "one another" responsibilities, many of which will be fulfilled individually, occur within the context of the congregation's corporate responsibility for itself. I mentioned above the elders' leadership role in accountability and discipline. But the New Testament ultimately charges the gathered congregation with responsibility for ensuring that members live up to their professions of faith and covenants with each other. Jesus does this in Matthew 18. Paul, too, exhorts not the pastors but the congregation to exclude an unrepentant man from membership (1 Corinthians 5). And he exhorts the congregation to restore someone who proves repentant (2 Cor. 2:6). This corporate congregational responsibility is both a part of discipling and itself an aid to the work of one-on-one discipling.

Let me illustrate. Suppose I have two Christian friends, one who is a member of my church and one who is not, and I am trying to disciple both of them. With the brother who is a member of my church, I can appeal to Sunday's sermon. I can appeal to the example set by our elders. I can appeal, if I must, to the threat of discipline for unrepentant sin. Plus, I know I'm personally responsible, *as a part of my corporate responsibility*, for pursuing the brother in all of these ways. And the fact that our discipling relationship occurs within this accountability context invigorates my sense of ownership and care. I'm responsible for him, just like I'm more responsible for my wife than for other women, or more responsible for my children than for other children.

Now with the brother who is *not* a member of my church, I am responsible, for Christ's sake, to love and encourage and warn him of the consequences of unrepentant sin. But I'm not the one tasked by Jesus with providing the final accountability structure in his life. The members of *his* church are. I wouldn't want to say that that fact will make me more complacent in my care for him. But it does lower the stakes and lessen my responsibility for him, again, just as I am less responsible for your children than I am for my own. Do you see how the church's responsibility for itself aids the work of discipling? Do you see how the skeleton of the body and the body's flesh and muscle hang together?

Formalizing our obligations to one another as a congregation helps us to commit to each person who joins the church. It aids our sense of ownership and responsibility. It gives form and shape to our discipling relationships.

A CULTURE OF DISCIPLING

Ultimately, our corporate responsibilities and our individual responsibilities blend together in a culture of discipling. We read and speak the Word to each other. We spend time with each other. We pray for the elders and one another. We love. We give. We attend the weekly gathering prayerfully and with anticipation. We come prepared. We plow up our hearts beforehand, ready to receive God's Word. We follow the example of our leaders who show us how to follow Christ ourselves. We submit to the wise leadership of the elders unless they are leading us in the wrong direction. We respect the stewardship the congregation has of us. We counsel and encourage and warn one another. "Let no corrupting talk come out of your mouths, but only such as is good for building up, as fits the occasion, that it may give grace to those who hear" (Eph. 4:29).

In the life of a church, spiritual growth and health should be the norm. It should be normal to see people growing and maturing spiritually. In fact, spiritual growth is not optional for the Christian; it indicates life. Things that are truly alive grow. Dead things don't. God has gifted a church with elders for the purposes of growth, and he has given us one another. It's within the context of all these relationships with members and pastors alike, all covenanted together, that we find the richest soil (along with the Christian family) for discipling relationships to (super)naturally grow. Our doctrine and life attain their shape within the doctrine and life of the community. This is a culture of discipling.

Are you struggling in your personal evangelism? Then I hope you will listen for the help, and prayer, and testimonies of other members of your church.

Are you enjoying your marriage right now or struggling in it? The local church is where to look for encouragement and counsel. It's where we receive instruction and give it, as we disciple each other.

How can an older member persevere in following Christ after a difficult surgery? Partly through a church's encouragement and love.

How can a younger Christian navigate his own discouragement and doubt when a friend walks away from the faith? Through the church's support and counsel.

How are we to find a spouse and rear a family, to be a good

67

employee and a faithful neighbor? Through the teaching of the local church, and the discipling that we find there.

How are other churches started and encouraged? How are Christian homes founded and nourished? How are ministries and opportunities for service shared? How are the weak strengthened, the straying sought, the evangelists stirred up? All through the local church!

In these ways and more we help one another follow Jesus. We disciple one another. Churches don't need programs so much as they need cultures of discipling, cultures where each member prioritizes the spiritual health of others. Each has been given a gift for the common good, and each should use whatever gift he or she has been given to build up the body: "Now there are varieties of gifts, but the same Spirit; and there are varieties of service, but the same Lord; and there are varieties of activities, but it is the same God who empowers them all in everyone. To each is given the manifestation of the Spirit for the common good" (1 Cor. 12:4–7).

In my own congregation, I pray and work for such a culture. I pray that through my own teaching ministry, as well as through the ministry of every member, we are all encouraged to share the gospel with our neighbors, to bear each others' burdens, to feel motivated to give financially to God's work, to give serious attention to God's Word, and to care and pray for the unity of those who have little in common apart from Christ.

THE LOCAL CHURCH IS BETTER

The local church—this Father-designed, Jesus-authorized, and Spirit-gifted body—is far better equipped to undertake the work of discipling believers than simply you and your one friend. Jesus does not promise that you and your one friend will defeat the gates of hell. He promises that the church will do this. You cannot recognize yourself as gifted and called to teach God's Word, or to baptize and administer the Lord's Supper, like a local church is so authorized.

Suppose that tomorrow a non-Christian friend of yours in another city for whom you've been praying for years becomes a Christian and starts attending an evangelical church in his city. How would you want that church to receive your friend, whom you love? Presumably, you'd want the congregation as a whole to take responsibility for him. You'd want the elders to teach him. And you'd want a number of individuals in particular to reach out to him, to take him under their wing, to disciple him. You'd want them to teach and model what it means to study the Bible, to walk in righteousness, to evangelize, to be a Christian spouse and parent, to stand up to the world, and to disciple others in turn. And how you would rejoice if that church took responsibility for your friend like this, no?

Now, do you receive and disciple the members of your church like this? Have you been helping others follow Jesus? Are you the answer to prayer of Christians in other cities?

If not, don't panic. I'm not going to ask you to start discipling dozens. Instead, I want you to think about one person in your church—just one. Think of one person whom you would love to see following Jesus more. Now, pray for that person . . .

Did you pray? Next, how do you think you might go about discipling that person?

Okay, maybe that word *discipling* still seems intimidating

to you. Let me rephrase: how do you think you might go about helping that person follow Jesus? Or, how can you do deliberate spiritual good in his or her life? What are one or two small steps you can take?

We turn to the "how" question of discipling in our next section.

7

CHOOSE SOMEONE

Imagine two church members. Let's call them Bob and Bill. Bob is a Bible student. He likes to know what the Bible says about everything. He can even explain the doctrine of the Trinity if you ask him to. Some of his actions may not seem to show he's a Christian. In fact, his life doesn't seem very Christian at all. But he knows his Bible!

Then there's Bill. Bill doesn't advertise the fact but he doesn't read his Bible much. Certainly he wants to be "good." He tries to love others. But Bill would have a hard time offering an orthodox explanation of who Jesus is, or what the church is. And he wouldn't do so well defining ethical issues carefully. But he means to live differently than the selfish, self-consumed life he sees others living. He likes to think of himself as a relationship guy rather than a Bible guy or doctrine guy.

Do either of these individuals sound like you?

Bob should care more about people, and Bill should care more about truth. Really, both should care more about Jesus, because Jesus loves the truths of God's Word and the lives of God's people. And the discipling work of a church should help both kinds of people better follow Jesus. Jesus said that whoever would "come after me, let him deny himself and take up his cross and follow me" (Mark 8:34). Bob needs to deny himself and follow Jesus by loving people more. Bill must do this by working to love God's Word more. A disciple is not someone who merely claims to follow Christ. He really does.

That's where any conversation about discipling others must begin—in remembering what it means to follow Jesus. Discipling means helping others follow Jesus. Discipling is a relationship in which we seek to do spiritual good for someone by initiating, teaching, correcting, modeling, loving, humbling ourselves, counseling, and influencing.

How then do we disciple? How exactly do we help Bob care more about living out his faith, and Bill care more about understanding it? That's the question we will consider for this and the next couple of chapters.

It's not just a question for pastors. The Bible tasks all of us with this kind of work. John tells us to love one another (2 John 5). Paul tells us to encourage one another and build one another up (1 Thess. 5:11). He also tells us to instruct one another, since we want to see everyone mature in Christ (Col. 1:28). The author of Hebrews tells us to consider how to stir one another up to love and good works (Heb. 10:24).

The first matter you will have to decide is, who should you spend time with? You only have so much time in the week. You cannot disciple the whole church. How do you decide in whom to invest? You have to choose.

With Bible in hand, how should we go about deciding in whom to invest? Here are nine factors to consider, and probably in this order.

1. FAMILY MEMBER

Paul writes, "If anyone does not provide for his relatives, and especially for members of his household, he has denied the faith and is worse than an unbeliever" (1 Tim. 5:8). The Bible teaches in this passage and others that each of us possesses a special responsibility for the members of our own family. In the family, God gives life-long relationships and natural grounds for affection and concern. And those natural affections and responsibilities should be employed for Christward ends. That's especially the case if you live with these family members. It's even more the case if Scripture charges you with special responsibility for them, as it does for parents with children or spouses for each other. These relationships are the most important discipling charge you have.

2. SPIRITUAL STATE

You should evangelize your non-Christian friends, but it is pointless to disciple them as if they are Christians. Paul tells us, "The natural person does not accept the things of the Spirit of God, for they are folly to him, and he is not able to understand them because they are spiritually discerned" (1 Cor. 2:14). You want to disciple a Christian.

3. CHURCH MEMBERSHIP

Back in chapter 6, we considered these charges from the book of Hebrews:

> Remember your leaders, those who spoke to you the word of God. Consider the outcome of their way of life and imitate their

> faith. . . . Obey your leaders and submit to them, for they are
> keeping watch over you souls, as those who will have to give an
> account. Let them do this with joy and not with groaning, for
> that would be of no advantage to you. (Heb. 13:7, 17)

Certainly these verses call us to particularly heed the leaders
of our own churches. Yet a further implication is that the ordinary pathways of discipleship work best within the relational
context of one's church, as argued in earlier chapters.

We have a greater responsibility for our own congregation—to help them and be helped by them. Members of the
same church follow and submit to the same body of elders.
They affirm the same statement of faith and church covenant.
They experience the same teaching on primary and secondary
matters. They see each other at least weekly. For all of these
reasons, it is normally more expedient to build discipling relationships within the context of one's church.

Furthermore, if a friend of yours attends an unhealthy
church, you might be doing damage to their spiritual life by
discipling them. How? Your spiritual support, ironically, en-
ables him or her to remain in a church that does not teach the
Bible. This is not an absolute rule, but it may be better just
to encourage your friend to join a healthy church. Christians
need the whole body, not just you.

4. GENDER

Scripture is sensitive to matters of gender in discipling. For
instance, Paul tells Titus, "Older women . . . are to teach what
is good, and so train the young women to love their husbands

and children, to be self-controlled, pure, working at home, kind, and submissive to their own husbands, that the word of God may not be reviled" (Titus 2:3–5).

In public settings, I teach men and women. Plus, we all have a mother and father, and many of us have sisters or brothers, or spouses. Which is to say, discipling the opposite sex is built into our families. And in the church we covenant together with men and women and have family friends.

Yet when it comes to a normal, deliberate discipling relationship, it is wise for men to disciple men and women to disciple women. We recognize that gender is a God-given reality, and we mean to treat it realistically and respectfully. We should love everyone in the church, and at the same time labor to avoid wrong intimacies.

5. AGE

Just as Scripture is sensitive to gender, so it's sensitive to age. In the Titus passage just mentioned, younger women learn from the older. Elsewhere Paul tells Timothy to not allow his youth to be despised, yet in the same letter he encourages Timothy to respect older men (1 Tim. 4:12; 5:1).

Normally you would disciple someone younger than yourself. Having said that, Scripture is full of exceptional examples of the younger teaching the older. And surely, as we advance in age, we also want to advance in the humility of learning from those of our own age, and even those younger than us. Otherwise, we will have no teachers left! Personally, I find I learn much from friends in their twenties and thirties, even as I do from folks in their seventies and eighties.

6. DIFFERENT FROM YOU

Few things visibly display the power of the gospel as much as the unity it achieves among people divided by the categories of this world. "For through [Christ]," observes the book of Ephesians, "we both [Jews and Gentiles] have access in one Spirit to the Father" (Eph. 2:18). The dividing wall of partition between Jew and Gentile fell at the cross. And now the wisdom of God is displayed through the unity of these formally divided people (Eph. 3:10). And of course the unity that the church experiences now across ethnic, economic, education, and other kinds of divides anticipates that day when "a great multitude that no one could number, from every nation, from all tribes and peoples and languages," stand perfectly together before God's throne in worship (Rev. 7:9–10).

What does this mean practically? As you look for someone to disciple, by all means the middle-aged mothers should befriend each other; and young married couples should spend time together; and single men in their twenties should hang out. Such groups have things in common that God can use for growth. *But also* consider what you might learn by spending time with college students; or working with the children and youth; or helping internationals from England and Brazil and Korea; or, if you are a young white husband, meeting with an older African-American husband.

How much God has to teach us about himself from people who are different from us! And how the gospel is displayed in our unity—not just the unity of liking each other, but the unity of learning from one another.

7. TEACHABILITY

Proverbs again and again commends the teachable son and repudiates the fool who scorns rebuke, instruction, and counsel. Furthermore, it tells us that God "leads the humble in what is right, and teaches the humble his way" (Ps. 25:9; cf. Prov. 11:2). Therefore, Peter instructs, "Likewise, you who are younger, be subject to the elders. Clothe yourselves, all of you, with humility toward one another, for 'God opposes the proud but gives grace to the humble'" (1 Pet. 5:5).

You don't want to spend time trying to teach someone who thinks you have nothing to teach them, and that they have nothing to learn. Teach the teachable. And try to be teachable yourself.

8. FAITHFULNESS TO TEACH OTHERS

I've also mentioned Paul's words to Timothy a couple of times now: "What you have heard from me in the presence of many witnesses entrust to faithful men who will be able to teach others also" (2 Tim. 2:2).

We want to disciple everyone, and we especially want to disciple those who will turn and disciple those who will disciple others. We will do addition if we have to, but we'd really like to do multiplication. We are not simply mentoring the next generation; we are trying to reach all generations to come!

9. PROXIMITY AND SCHEDULES

Finally, believe it or not, the Bible is sensitive to time and our busy schedules. Paul writes, "So then, *as we have oppor-*

tunity, let us do good to everyone, and especially to those who are of the household of faith" (Gal. 6:10). You'll find a number of other verses like this one, calling us to make the best use of our time (e.g., Eph. 5:16). This final characteristic I'm talking about is a matter of wisdom. But generally I'd recommend finding those whose schedules align with your own. You must also consider where you live or work, and your time commitments with family, job, and church. Assume that God isn't calling you to do something impossible.

In all of this, of course, God prepares the good works in advance for us to do (Eph. 2:10). And as with the Good Samaritan, sometimes he places people in our path who we might not ordinarily think to spend time with. Maybe it's a member of your church who happens to work in your office, or whose children participate in the same sporting events as your children. Or maybe someone's spouse leaves, and the grieving party turns to you.

All that to say, be wise and thoughtful about whom you choose to spend time with, but know that the Lord's providence sometimes overrules all our planning. Praise God, it keeps us dependent upon him!

PUTTING IT TOGETHER

Suppose your schedule only permits you to spend time with Bob or Bill, but not both. How do you choose? Certainly you should pray about it, but there's no necessarily right answer, and you should not feel guilty if you are unable to spend time with both. This is why we have the body of Christ.

You might choose to spend time with Bob because his

work schedule better matches yours or because he lives in your neighborhood or your wives are already good friends. You might decide to pour into Bill because he will be moving back to Bogota, Colombia, next summer, he shows a penchant for teaching others, and you want to equip him to equip others in Bogota. Whatever the rationale, pray, ask for wisdom, and then get to it.

In all of this, whether you are self-consciously discipling one person or four, make sure that you are growing spiritually, and then help those around you to grow. Both are important, and each contributes to the other.

8

HAVE CLEAR AIMS

Once you choose someone to disciple, have clear aims for that relationship. The larger goal, of course, is to help him or her follow Jesus. But how specifically are you going to do that? Discipling a truth person like Bob will look different than discipling a relationship person like Bill (our two characters from the last chapter).

That said, let me encourage you to always think both in terms of what people understand and how they live.

HELP PEOPLE TO UNDERSTAND MORE: LIFE→TRUTH→LIFE

For starters, your discipling should help people *understand more*. We want people to grow in the knowledge of God in Christ, and faith comes from hearing the word of Christ. Paul therefore tells Timothy to keep a close watch on himself and *on the teaching*. By persisting in this, Paul says, Timothy will save both himself and his hearers (1 Tim. 4:16).

Through discipling, you want people to know why Christians pray, why we share the gospel, why we join a church, why knowledge of God's sovereignty impacts how we live, and more. Discipling is not merely about accountability and behavior modification. Jesus tells us to make disciples by teaching people to obey, but they cannot obey what they haven't been taught. We first have to teach.

The Word of God should be central to any discipling relationship. Discipling might therefore involve outlining a book of the Bible with someone or studying the Word in some other fashion. We're to help one another "hold fast to the word of life," as Paul put it (Phil. 2:16). What a great phrase! Encourage people to hold fast to the Word of life by reading and understanding and obeying. You might use good Christian books in a discipling relationship, yet the best books take people to the Bible. We want the basics of the Christian faith and life to be clearly understood.

Have you ever heard of the *life→truth→life* pattern? Your *life* should attract people to listen to you; your *teaching* should then work for their transformation; their transformed *lives* should then illustrate what you taught, which in turn attracts people to listen to them.

HELP PEOPLE TO LIVE BETTER

We don't only want to help people understand better, we also want to help them *to live better*. Following Christ includes both. Again and again Paul calls his readers to imitate him as he imitates Christ (1 Cor. 4:15–17; 11:1; Phil. 3:17; 4:9; 2 Thess. 3:7–9; 2 Tim. 3:10–11). And of course he is imitating Jesus in this. Jesus calls his disciples to love as he loved (John 13:35; 15:8–17)!

Knowing God changes how we live (see Gal. 4:9). We live as aliens and strangers in an antagonistic world, always faced with the pressure to conform. But the Bible calls us to resist that pressure. We are to be "blameless and innocent, children of God without blemish in the midst of a crooked and twisted generation, among whom you shine as lights in the world" (Phil. 2:15). This is why Christians always need better examples of godliness set before them: "Brothers, join in imitating me, and keep your eyes on those who walk according to the example you have in us" (Phil. 3:17).

How then do you impact how others live? By spending time with them. Elizabeth invites Kate over to talk while she does her baking. Michael has Steven join his family for dinner, and then lets him watch as he leads his children in family worship. So much of discipling is doing what you ordinarily do but bringing people along with you and having meaningful conversations, like Jesus did. And when you invite them into your life, be transparent. Facades defeat the purpose. Invite others to learn from your mistakes.

The truth is, my wife and I argue sometimes. But can we do that well? Can we share those struggles with others without dishonoring each other?

Listen to how Paul involved Timothy in everything: "You, however, have followed my teaching, my conduct, my aim in life, my faith, my patience, my love, my steadfastness, my persecutions and sufferings that happened to me at Antioch, at Iconium, and at Lystra—which persecutions I endured" (2 Tim. 3:10–11). Timothy, apparently, saw it all. And what a rich education in following Christ it must have been!

You want the people you disciple to prosper in prayer, to improve in evangelism, to continue in church membership, to forbear with the members who offend them. So often, it will be the sermon preached the previous week that will allow you to work out these kinds of implications in one another's lives. Small groups can do the same.

ASK QUESTIONS

No matter who you disciple, you want to help them better follow Jesus by growing in the knowledge of God and by learning to put that knowledge into practice—to understand better and to live better.

Beyond that, of course, so much depends on the specific person: what are his or her interests, backgrounds, proclivities, sin patterns, hurts, fears, hopes, and more. And the kind of things you talk about, or read, or do, will depend on the person. Therefore one of the first things you should do in a discipling relationship is get to know the person by asking lots of questions. How did you become a Christian? Where are you from? Were your parents Christians? Your grandparents? Why do you have the job that you do? And so forth. In time, the level of trust and transparency should grow, and more and more you should be able to talk about the deeper, more personal matters and what the gospel means in those areas.

Really, the "how" of discipling is not that complicated. It's about doing life together with other people as you all journey toward Christ. We make friends and then walk them in a Christward direction. We want to understand God and his ways and live as the Bible calls us to. We want to be accurate in our understanding and holy in our living. We want to know the truth and to live well. All to the glory of the God in whose image we're made!

9

PAY THE COST

How do you disciple? You find someone. You establish goals. And finally, you just do it. You disciple. And to do that, you have to pay the cost. The cost is time, study, prayer, and love.

1. DISCIPLING TAKES TIME

When I say "discipling," I should be clear that not all discipling relationships look the same. Mine don't. They conform to the circumstances of my life and the other person's life. And those relationships change over time. I may see someone almost every day for a while, then every week, then once a month. Also, these relationships can fall anywhere on a spectrum between more and less formal. Even whether you call any given relationship a "discipling relationship" doesn't matter. But what all of these relationships have in common is that they take time!

It's the cost of time that requires us to be deliberate about discipling someone. And time limits the number of discipling relationships we can have. Yes, you can disciple lots of people by preaching a sermon or writing an article, but here we are talking about one-to-one or small group discipling. And these must be deliberate and intentional.

Even if your schedules work together, discipling relationships take time. Convenience will not entirely eliminate cost. Anytime we do life-on-life relationships, we give each other the gift of time. You can pay that cost in small ways, like talking to others after church or running errands with each other. You can pay it in larger ways, like scheduling weekly meals together. We can spend time together in a variety of ways: in a coffee shop, at a library, at an auto repair shop, or during yard work.

You may find that some people are so willing to spend time with you that they'll fold into your life or serve you or your family. You help to make the time worthwhile by being transparent and honest in the relationship. As I've suggested already, our examples of enduring hardship are often more powerful than our stories of success and triumph. Trials expose what our hearts truly trust in, and what our hopes are. Time passing in a fallen world always brings trials. Trials are key times in discipling relationships, whether the trial is in the life of the one discipling or the one being discipled.

And beware: if you wait to build these relationships until you need them, it may be too late.

2. DISCIPLING REQUIRES STUDY

If faith comes by hearing the Word, we want to feed faith with the Word. The expositional sermons you hear preached at church (I hope) provide good foundations for conversations the following week. Other books can help as well, as they lead you deeper into a topic.

We study the things we love. My friend Sebastian, when he was seven, had his mother quiz him on baseball statistics using his baseball cards like memory flashcards. Clearly he loved baseball. Should those who love Jesus and intend to follow after him show less zeal? Christian discipleship and discipling involves loving God with our minds. We should desire to know him, and help others know him, as he has revealed himself in the Word.

In your discipling relationships, use the Bible. Spend time in the Word.

3. DISCIPLING REQUIRES PRAYER

Paul tells us to "pray without ceasing" (1 Thess. 5:17). Pray for those you're discipling and teach them to pray. The changes we need are supernatural changes, even if God uses human means like prayer.

In your discipling, ask questions that help people think through what they pray about. Do they know how to take a passage of Scripture and pray from it? Are they spending personal time in prayer? What kind of things do they pray about? Who are they praying for? Do they pray about friendships? About ministry? About money? About friends they would like to be converted? About their own purity and holiness?

Read good books that demonstrate how to pray from Scripture, such as D. A. Carson's *Praying with Paul* and Donald Whitney's *Praying the Bible*. And pray.

4. DISCIPLING REQUIRES LOVE

Jesus instructs, "Just as I have loved you, you also are to love one another" (John 13:34). He also summarizes the whole law in the two commands to love God and to love your neighbor as yourself (Mark 12:28–31). Hopefully, you see how important love is in a discipling relationship.

Love initiates a discipling relationship. Why else would we begin? It is love that constrains us to deny ourselves and serve others. It is love that causes us to risk being rejected, which is always a threat when starting a relationship. It is always love for God and others that leads us to overlook the difficulties and absorb the costs because we want to see someone grow.

Love perseveres in a discipling relationship. Why else besides love would we endure the challenges that come! "He's taking me for granted." "She doesn't see how saying that hurt me!" "I'm too busy." Discipling relationships can be great, but even great relationships take a persevering love, as in marriage. Of course this requires us to recall how radically and completely we've been loved by God. And that love spills over, and keeps spilling over.

Love humbly receives the criticism that often comes in a discipling relationship. Love and vanity don't work well together. If I'm concerned only with what the other person thinks of me instead of with how he or she is doing, it will be hard for me to love and disciple as I should. I won't be able speak or to receive the corrective word in season. To do that, my love for God and my friend must exceed my love for my own reputation. "Faithful are the wounds of a friend" (Prov. 27:6).

Love humbly gives of itself in a discipling relationship. Maybe you're tempted to think that you're too big, too important, too busy to love this other person. There is a place to consider your schedule, to be sure. But love will enable you to value the other person as you should, and so give of yourself. We build relational capital in order to spend it for the good of those we love.

Love allows us to end discipling relationships. We are not God. We cannot provide everything someone needs. We might not always be available. People move. Another child is born. You get a different job. Circumstances change. Maybe they need something that you are not equipped to give. We need a love that humbles us enough to recognize that what they need is not us, but God, and that God can use us for a while, and then use someone else.

CONCLUSION

Each one of us is called to love and be loved. Everything the Lord gives you, he means for you to turn around and give to others in some form or fashion. Any time, truth, prayer, or love he gives you can be used for others.

Richard Sibbes once wrote, "We must one day give an account to God, not only for what sermons we have heard, but for the examples of those amongst whom we have lived."[1] Could it be that in our evangelical churches today, we have been primarily providing words? Good, true, and needed words, and yet words that are, by themselves, incomplete without the lives that explain and demonstrate their meaning?

Whatever church you attend, the opportunities for discipling are immense! You even have the opportunity to impact the people who attend your church for a short time, so that when they leave, they can extend your ministry into another church. Discipling has its challenges and costs, to be sure. Yet God gets the glory in all of this!

10

RAISING UP LEADERS

The New Testament is filled with instruction on discipling believers generally. But now and then it also focuses on raising up church leaders in particular. For instance, Paul tells Titus, "This is why I left you in Crete, so that you might put what remained into order and appoint elders in every town as I directed you" (Titus 1:5). Then he describes what these elders should be like. Similarly, he tells Timothy to find "faithful men who will be able to teach others also" (2 Tim. 2:2).

In the same way, I'd like to conclude this book by offering counsel on how I have personally worked to find, encourage, and raise up other leaders in my church, whether to serve in my church or eventually in other churches. Many of the matters discussed below apply to discipling more broadly. After all, the criteria listed for an elder in Titus 1 and 1 Timothy 3 should characterize every Christian, with the exception of not being a recent convert and being able to teach. Which is to say, the goals of discipling a believer and a would-be church leader are mostly the same. We seek maturity in Christ. So I hope and trust the following material will be helpful for every reader.

Still, I do want to lay the onus on elders especially to think about how to raise up future leaders. That is one of your particular obligations. Samuel Miller once observed,

> Wherever you reside, endeavor always to acquire and maintain an influence with young men. They are the hope of the church and of the state; and he who becomes instrumental in imbuing their minds with sentiments of wisdom, virtue and piety, is one of the greatest benefactors of his species. They are, therefore, worthy of your special and unwearied attention. . . . In short, employ every Christian method of attaching them to your person and ministry, and of inducing them to take an early interest in the affairs of the church.[1]

Here then are nine steps for raising up church leaders.

1. SHEPHERD TOWARD BIBLICAL QUALIFICATIONS

The place to begin is with the qualifications that Paul gives to Timothy and Titus:

> If anyone aspires to the office of overseer, he desires a noble task. Therefore an overseer must be above reproach, the husband of one wife, sober-minded, self-controlled, respectable, hospitable, able to teach, not a drunkard, not violent but gentle, not quarrelsome, not a lover of money. He must manage his own household well, with all dignity keeping his children submissive, for if someone does not know how to manage his own household, how will he care for God's church? He must not be a recent convert, or he may become puffed up with conceit and fall into the condemnation of the devil. Moreover, he must be well thought of by outsiders, so that he may not fall into disgrace, into a snare of the devil. (1 Tim. 3:1–7; also, Titus 1:6–9)

There is nothing extraordinary about these virtues. But as I heard D. A. Carson once say, an elder does what an ordinary Christian should do extraordinarily well. He is a model for the whole flock. He is a picture of maturity for all of them.

I will occasionally ask young men whether they have thought about serving as an elder, and I will do that early on in their discipleship, knowing that they may be years away from being qualified and ready. It's my way of asking whether serving and building up the church is one of their ambitions, and if not, why not? Which is to say, a good discipling tool for *every* Christian is this list (with the exception of able to teach).

That said, I don't believe Paul means to provide an exhaustive list for what an elder should be in these lists. For instance, he never says "faithful Bible reader" or "man of prayer," though I think every elder should be those two things. When it comes to raising up leaders generally, and men whom the church would financially support especially, I do think we should also look for natural gifts of leadership. I want to promote and equip men who look like they can help to advance Christianity into the place I'll never go: the future beyond my passing.

Does this mean I'm transgressing James 2:1 and playing favorites? I don't think so. James is concerned with wrongly favoring the rich. But such wrong discernment and discrimination doesn't make all distinctions wrong. Remember, Paul tells Timothy to look for "faithful men" who can "teach others," as well as men who "aspire to the office of overseer." A man can aspire for the wrong reasons, but a man who doesn't aspire at all is not qualified.

Ultimately, you want to shepherd men toward biblical

qualified-ness. That's the baseline. And the more a man also demonstrates the natural giftings, which show themselves in the fact that people follow him, the more you might look for opportunities to have him practice leading.

2. ADOPT A POSTURE OF LOOKING

If you want to raise up leaders, you need to be on permanent lookout for more leaders. This should be your posture, especially if you are an elder. Sydney Anglican Phillip Jenson refers to "blokes worth watching." Can you name any BWWs around you?

Pastors should be profoundly opportunistic about raising up more pastors. And the whole church should have a deep confidence that the Lord wants new leaders raised up.

I keep my eyes open in a number of ways. I hang around the congregation and interact with them. I stand at the door after Sunday services and notice who says what, or who is interacting with whom. I work to provide lots of teaching opportunities in the weekly life of our church where gifted teachers can emerge. Praying daily through the church's membership directory also brings people to mind.

3. SPEND PERSONAL TIME

Spending time with people is a crucial part of raising up leaders. Earlier in the book I mentioned Jesus calling the disciples to join him on the mountain so that they might "be with him."

Sadly, I see pastors build walls around themselves. Those are not men who will be raising up more leaders, at least directly. I'm not saying you need to be an extrovert, but a pastor does need to find some way to spend time with other potential leaders in his church. Hebrews 13 exhorts the church to follow an elder's example. How can they do that if they don't know their leaders up close? Paul's call to imitation requires the same—time spent.

So a pastor needs to figure out ways to spend time with younger men. Lunches can be crucial. On those occasions when my wife asks me to go the grocery store, I typically break into a cold sweat for fear of getting the wrong thing (my issues, not hers!), and so I often bring a brother with me. That way, we can spend intentional time together, and he can share the blame. I build people into my sermon preparation schedule, too, including a lunch devoted to brainstorming over application and a Saturday night reading preview. Not only do these encounters improve the sermon, but I'm also able to get a sense of different folks, and encourage them.

All these examples are designed around me, my work, and my schedule. Figure out what schedule works for you, and draw disciples into it.

4. ADVANCE TRUST

If you want to see leaders raised up, your general posture should be characterized by a willingness to advance trust. Based on living in different places and traveling, I know such a disposition varies from place to place. But I do think it's a property of love: love believes all things, hopes all things (1 Cor. 13:7). You probably have members of your church whom the Lord has entrusted with great talent. But for that to be discovered, someone must advance trust to them, like credit. And good leaders do this. They don't wait for people to prove themselves, and then give them teaching opportunities. No, they see the hint of something that, with a little encouragement, could grow and flourish. So they advance credit and let the young disciple spend it!

Many leaders, with the best of motives, can be too conservative here. More than once I have seen senior pastors unable to affirm anyone else's leadership. Or I have witnessed men become lay elders and then pull the tree house rope ladder up after them, so that no one else can get in, asking more of prospective elders than anyone ever asked of them! Now, you will make mistakes. You will not bat a thousand. I haven't. But I do definitely take risks in leadership. It's worth it. Christ will build his church. God is sovereign. So we should lean in and take some risks.

Congregations, for their part, need to be patient with young men in leadership as they make young-man mistakes. I often tell churches not to be afraid of nominating a young lion cub. He may scratch the floors or damage some furniture, but if you're patient with him, you'll have a lion who loves you for life.

5. DELEGATE RESPONSIBILITY

This point is tied to the last one. How do you advance trust? By delegating responsibility and opportunity. There are several components to this:

Give people the opportunity to lead. Quietly keep a list of men in your congregation that you think might be good teachers, or public prayers, or service leaders, or Sunday school teachers. Test them by delegating. Again, I recognize that some pastors feel very protective about their flocks: "But Mark, the Holy Spirit has made *me* the overseer" (see Acts 20:28). That's where I say, when you die, friend, the church is going to be fine! And you want to help make it *more fine* by loosening your grip now and preparing other leaders by delegating. Your goal is not to build your kingdom; you empower by giving others opportunities to lead and teach.

Lose votes and arguments. Delegating authority means ceding a measure of control, and if you are willing to do that, you need to be willing to lose votes or not always have the last word. Not everything must go your way. If you never let people lead in a way contrary to your own opinion, *you are not really letting them lead!* So, yes, you might be disappointed to lose on this or that issue, but the gain of encouraging other leaders to lead is a better long-term investment (not to mention blessing the church by the gifts of their wisdom).

Cultivate respect for other leaders. Some years ago, our assistant pastor and I were standing on the platform at the front of the church before a Bible study started. He was about to lead it. In the midst of talking playfully with each other, I patted him on the head (he's shorter than I am). He immediately took me aside and said, kindly but firmly, "Mark, stop it. You can't treat me like that in front of the congregation if you want them to respect me." Once he said it, it seemed so obvious. Of course! I needed to treat him publicly like a leader and work to cultivate that respect for him in the congregation.

6. GIVE FEEDBACK

Once you delegate responsibilities and opportunities to minister, you also need to create structures for feedback. For starters, that means showing those you are discipling how to give and receive godly criticism. Be honest and tender with brothers about things they could improve upon.

Your ability to give godly criticism will be greatly enhanced by modeling what it means to invite and receive godly criticism. To encourage that, I try to receive critical comments without answering back (not that I always succeed), even if I disagree with the criticism. I do answer if I think the comment will mislead others, but if I slap down every constructive criticism a younger man offers me, especially after I have invited the feedback, he'll quickly learn that it's futile (and embarrassing) for him to offer forthright opinions to me. And that will prove the least useful for me! There is always room for improvement in my ministry. The feedback I have received for twenty years has greatly helped me to serve the church better.

In addition to modeling what it means to give and receive godly criticism, we must also model giving godly encouragement. Paul had plenty of critical things to say to the Corinthian church, yet he opens the letter by giving thanks to God for them, "that in every way [they] were enriched in him in all speech and all knowledge so that [they were] not lacking in any gift" (1 Cor. 1:5, 7). I don't think that Paul was flattering the Corinthians. I think he was rightly acknowledging what God had done. Should we not acknowledge that what comes from God belongs to God, like the evidences of grace in one another's lives? Encouraging would-be leaders should teach them to give praise *to God*.

So many times I've seen men, particularly younger guys, act as if real leadership is shown in correcting others. That's why young men's sermons often scold. What they haven't figured out is that you can often accomplish more by encouragement. There are times to scold. But 80 to 90 percent of what you hope to correct can be accomplished through encouragement. If you look back at your life and consider who influenced you the most, you will probably find that it's the people who believed in you. Henry Drummond once observed: "You will find, if you think for a moment, that the people who influence you are people who believe in you. In an atmosphere of suspicion men shrivel up; but in that atmosphere they expand, and find encouragement and educative fellowship."[2]

When I observe that the men I'm discipling give encouragement and criticism to me or to one another, I learn as much about them as I do about the thing they are commenting on. It's like standing in an art gallery and looking not at the paintings, but at the people observing the paintings. What are they drawn to? What do they emphasize? Setting up good feedback loops, if you are a pastor, helps all of this discipling to happen.

7. ENCOURAGE GODLY AUTHORITY

Too often, people today don't understand what a gift godly authority can be. Raising up leaders requires us to teach about godly authority, and encourage it. Jesus certainly taught his disciples about a right use of authority (Matt. 20:25–27).

The fallen world both misuses authority and lies about

authority well used. Satan's basic lie to Adam and Eve was that God couldn't really love them and tell them no.

When people are skittish over complementarianism, apologizing for it, I know they are probably thinking about authority in a wrong way. It's as if they think authority is only an advantage for the person who possesses it. Apparently they haven't had children! Authority looks like an advantage only to someone who doesn't have it. When you have the authority, pretty much all the "advantages" seem to vanish, and you begin to realize how much of it is service—a glorious service, but a service.

This became clear to me years ago when I was preaching through 2 Samuel. David's "last words" are striking: "When one rules justly over men, ruling in the fear of God, he dawns on them like the morning light, like the sun shining forth on a cloudless morning, like rain that makes grass to sprout from the earth" (23:3–4). Good authority blesses those under it. It nourishes them. People will gravitate toward good healthy authority that spends itself for the good of those under its care, rather than using them for its own good. Look at how a family prospers under good parents, or a team under a good coach.

That's why the abuse of authority by pastors is such a terribly destructive and blasphemous sin. Furthermore, the stories of prosperity preachers buying private jets for tens of millions of dollars point to something incredibly twisted and Satanic. Such "pastors" play right into the lie that Satan hissed into Adam and Eve's ear in the garden of Eden: that authority is just a way to abuse you for the leader's benefit.

Gratefully, the King on the cross shows us that the opposite is true for godly authority.

Just as Jesus tutored his disciples in the godly use of authority, so must we with any men whom we are raising up in leadership. And pastors must model such authority.

8. EXPECT CLARITY

Leaders in the church must know how to be unusually clear on doctrine and in teaching the truth generally. This is an implication of what Paul teaches the Ephesian leaders in Acts 20. And it's his assumption throughout his letters to Timothy and Titus. For instance, he observes that "Adam was not deceived, but the woman was deceived and became a transgressor" (1 Tim. 2:14). A leader must possess a clear-headedness about the truth. You want people who have a natural ability to answer the question, "Why?" And they need to be especially clear about certain issues: the most basic matters of theology and the gospel; those doctrines that distinguish your church from others; and those teachings of the Bible that are under fire and currently unpopular in the world at large.

9. FOSTER A CULTURE OF HUMILITY

What all eight of these previous practices require is a culture of humility. Christian discipling depends on such humility, not envy.

It's no sign of humility in me if I'm watching someone else minister and thinking either "I could do better!" or, feeling discouraged, "I could never do it *that* well." God does different good things with different people. We're like different instruments in the orchestra, and a good leader helps each person find his or her place. Why would the trombone be jealous of the kettledrum? Each can be enjoyed for what it is.

Fostering a culture of humility means working against the fear of man. And we do that, of course, by learning to fear the Lord. Before men attend my church's pastoral internship, we ask them to read Ed Welch's *When People Are Big and God Is Small*. If you do not know that book, I highly commend it. Every would-be leader should learn to recognize fear of man in himself. One way we can see it in a new intern is when he shows up in our church and is threatened by other strong leaders. But I want strong leaders, as many as I can get. After all, one way to view my whole ministry is getting my church ready for the next pastor.

In general, humility leads us to speak when we should speak and stay silent when we should stay silent. It leads us to be both tenderhearted and thick-skinned. I want to see God's church prosper by seeing more humble leaders being raised up. And I think that my humility is part of how that will happen.

What a joy to be used by God to disciple others! Why would you not spend your life doing this?

CONCLUSION

by Jonathan Leeman

Throughout this book, Mark has sprinkled a few illustrations of how he has personally put some of his instructions into practice. What the reader misses, for self-evident reasons, is the great illustration that is his own life. Having known Mark for nearly two decades as a member of his church, and served with him for nearly ten years, that is a regret for me. I wish the reader could have seen what I have seen in order to put flesh on the principles you've encountered over the previous ten chapters.

Some of the things that Mark does in discipling are the properties of his personality and cannot be replicated. The good news for you and me is that the biblical material explored in this book can be. So also can the lessons on one theme that I would like to explore here. Those are lessons on the theme of authority.

I asked for—or really, took—the privilege of concluding this volume so that I can paint the illustration that is his life— to help you see what I see. In a single sentence, what Mark does unusually well, and what I would commend to you no matter your vocation or role in a church, is to combine these two things: *exercising authority* and *giving away authority*.

I suspect most people regard these activities as opposites, and in a fallen world they typically are. But anyone familiar with the life of Christ, and who understands how godly authority works generally, knows that *exercising authority* and *giving away authority* are two sides of the same coin.

You can guess at what I mean when I speak of *exercising authority*. It means a person treats the work to be done and the decisions to be made as belonging to him. He possesses decision-making power over some domain by moral right. And so he will take the initiative, take control, make decisions, and ensure the job gets done. This, to be sure, is Mark in his church. He leads. He steers the ship. It's the course he has charted together with the elders that our church follows. And there is no shyness or reticence in his leadership.

If a person exercises authority like this from a posture of pride, he will do all this insensitively at best, harshly at worst. He will treat people as means to his own ends, and they will not flourish or grow.

However, if a person leads like this from a posture of humility, he will *exercise authority* while also *giving away authority*. After all, he seeks not his own ends but the ends of the One who has put him in his office. So he will strive to equip and empower more people for the work. This, to be sure, is also Mark. He continually delegates, gives opportunity, and equips others to lead.

WAYS TO PASS OUT AUTHORITY

I will leave it to you, the reader, to figure out what passing out authority could look like in your discipling work, whether you are discipling in the home, the workplace, the Sunday school classroom, the small group, the parachurch ministry, the friendship, or any other domain. But let me list some ways I've seen Mark do it in his particular vocation of senior pastor (though I have converted his example to imperatives). The goal here is not to exalt Mark, but to say (as Paul says of himself), imitate him as he imitates Christ. I also hope you make this discovery: The work of discipling is about more than the one-on-one relationships that have been the focus of this book. Discipling, finally, is a lifestyle and way of living with others. It's about structuring all of your interactions in order to be *an exporter of opportunity*. Here, then, is how a pastor can do that, together with some questions for everyone in italics:

- Build the church on the gospel. No matter who's teaching, the gospel must be front and center. When relationships and power structures are grounded in the gospel, people use their authority not to lord it over one another, but to serve one another (Matt. 20:25–28). *Are you building your discipling relationship on the gospel or on performance?*
- Establish a plurality of staff and non-staff elders. On an elder board composed exclusively of staff elders, each man may possess one vote, but the staffing structure imposes a hierarchy. Adding non-staff elders to the board disrupts and flattens that hierarchy. *Do you give other people formal responsibility? Do you heed outside counsel in the domain of your expertise and authority?*
- Be willing to lose elder votes. I've heard of other senior pastors who "never lose votes." When that's the case, you almost might as well get rid of your elders. Talk about

undermining their leadership! *Do decisions always have to go your way?*

- Limit the percentage of main-slot preaching. Mark, with the elders' agreement, limits himself to preaching 50 to 65 percent of Sunday mornings. That way, other voices have the chance to grow and gain authority. And the congregation depends more on the Word than on one man. *Do you give someone you're discipling a chance to share the stage?*

- Create many other opportunities to teach. *Do you actively seek to create ministry opportunities for others?*

- Give young teachers the chance to make mistakes. I can think of one or two instances where a teacher or preacher said something so inappropriate that he wasn't asked to teach again. But generally speaking, young teachers have a lot of leeway in our church to be boring and to make mistakes. Since the church depends more on the Word than on Mark, they have much patience for the young men. *Are you a "one-strike you're out!" discipler, or do you give people a chance to make rookie mistakes?*

- Let others steal your ideas. Mark freely lets other teachers inside the church adapt his anecdotes, borrow his best lines, and mimic his messages. *Do you always have to get the credit?*

- Be slow to speak and speak sparingly in elders' meetings. *From choosing a restaurant to discussing a complex ethical issue, does your voice have to be the last voice in any conversation?*

- Don't be the chairman in elders' meetings or members' meetings. Giving another man the chance to be the chairman who both sets the agenda and also leads the meeting is an easy way to distribute authority. *Do you always have to be king, or do you also enjoy playing kingmaker?*

- Let other elders lead the congregation through difficult issues in members' meetings. When it comes to leading the church through discipline cases, big financial decisions, or other tough topics, the elder who's been most involved may be the best one to lead the church publicly. *Are you deeply aware of the fact that the Spirit has gifted the body of Christ with different gifts, and that each part of the body is needed, and that you are deeply dependent on the whole body? Does your leadership and discipling reflect this because you're constantly calling upon other people to lend their expertise and strengths?*

- Be devoted to one or two things in the church and give freedom elsewhere. Mark is largely devoted to preparing sermons and keeps a loose grip on most everything else. So if you want to see the church doing more in some area, he'll let you do it and keep his hands off. This process "outs" other natural leaders. *Do you take delight in strengths and talents that are not your own and encourage people in them? Or are you a trumpet player who cares only about the trumpet section and never bothers to enjoy and encourage the string section?*

- Don't micromanage. There are a few areas Mark micromanages, like making sure his staff are present at meetings and services on time. But in just about everything else, he gives free rein. Micromanagement not only exhausts a leader, it undermines the initiative of others. *Do you let others do and complete the job, even though you know you could do it better?*

- Be willing to receive criticism. Mark sets the example by inviting criticism. This gives other would-be leaders room to spread their wings. If you never invite criticism, you're teaching everyone around you that they must conform to your preferences or be punished. Leaders don't grow in this kind of environment. They wither or leave. *Do you invite critique? Do you say "thank you" when people answer, or do you argue?*

- Pray for other churches and other denominations. This defeats tribalism and focuses us on the gospel instead of the church leader. This prayer in turn engenders further gospel initiative among other budding leaders in the church. *Do you encourage the work of other people and teams that are pursuing the same ends as you? Or is everything about winning for you?*

- Be quick to forgive. It's hard for a fault-finder to give away authority. If you see only faults, you won't trust or entrust. But if you're quick to forgive, you'll find it easier to entrust and empower others. *Are you quick to forgive? Or do you quickly write people off?*

- Rejoice in the victories of others. Do you have to be the one to make the shot, or are you happy to make the assist? Mark rejoices in the victories of others as much as his own. If someone else can do the job, he would prefer it. This leaves him free to do something else. *How often do encouraging words come out of your mouth? How often do you congratulate someone else's performance, particularly when it's in your area of competence?*

Not all of these examples and questions translate neatly to a one-on-one discipling relationship, as I said. Rather, they point to an overall posture and lifestyle. And the posture is this: "God has given me a time and talent, and I'm going to use the best of my time and talent to equip and empower others. I'm not going to just tend my own garden. I'm going to help them tend theirs." What's more beautiful, after all: one nicely kept eight-by-eight garden plot filled with your roses? Or a whole patchwork quilt of eight-by-eight gardens filled with your roses, his tulips, her daisies, their begonias, lilies, irises, hydrangeas, carnations, and so much more?

HOW GIVING AWAY AUTHORITY SHAPES A CHURCH CULTURE

Think about what happens when the leader "on top" is characterized by generously giving authority to his lay elders and others in the church. Think about what happens when the members of a church all work to be exporters of opportunities. Think about what happens when you use your discipling relationships to give others authority. What happens? It shapes a church's culture in all sorts of wonderful ways. It plants and nourishes that patchwork quilt of beautiful gardens. Specifically,

1. It helps to keep the gospel uppermost. Giving away authority focuses the church's eyes on its gospel purposes rather than on the leader.

2. It promotes real relationships. In an environment where authority is jealously guarded, relationships are characterized by politics and strategy. Guards remain up, vulnerabilities aren't exposed, and transparency diminishes. But when people feel empowered, they're more likely to be open and honest.

3. It keeps a church from being tribalistic. People who continually give away authority teach those around them that they are most interested in the success of the gospel, regardless of who's leading (see Phil. 1:12–30).

4. It encourages church members to share resources. When I see that my leaders are not out for themselves, I too become inclined to give to others.

5. It destroys natural social hierarchies. Members interact as equals. Why? Because the gospel is kept in the center. We're all sinners saved by grace. The leaders don't lord it over others, and this sets a pattern for everyone.

6. It cultivates trust. When leaders and members aren't out for themselves, it's easier to trust their motives, even when they ask for sacrifices.

7. It cultivates teachability and the willingness to receive criticism. Again, if I trust the people who are over me (whether formally or informally), I become more willing to listen to their criticisms of me. I trust they're rooted in love rather than one-upmanship.

8. It promotes a willingness to forgive. When a leader is quick to forgive others' faults, he will be more willing to entrust others with authority. That in turn will help others to do the same.

9. It encourages the church to be training-minded. A church that sees its leaders continually work to train and empower others will have a hard time not catching the vision and sharing it.

10. It helps a church to be outward focused. The process of raising up leaders helps a church realize that its goal isn't just to make its own house the best it can be, but to help other houses become happier and healthier, too.

Sure, delegation can be done poorly or lazily. Wisdom is required to delegate well. The question comes down to heart posture: are we happy to see others gain authority, or do we jealously guard it, afraid people might surpass us? If the former, what are we doing to spread it?

Our supreme example of exercising authority while passing out authority is none other than God himself, particularly through the person of Jesus Christ. God created Adam in his image and "crowned" him with glory and dominion, putting everything under his feet (Ps. 8:5–6). He then gave Christ all authority in heaven and on earth in order to call out a people for himself (Matt. 28:18; cf. Heb. 2:6–8). Christ then commanded these people—us—to make disciples so that we might share in his reign. Astonishingly, the Bible even uses the language of a redeemed humanity reigning *with* God (in 2 Tim. 2:12; Rev. 20:6—literally, "be kings with").

If Christ for joy's sake would share his rule with us, how much joy do you expect we will find in sharing our rule with others? That, I think, is the heart of discipling: sharing rule. And what will be the result? Knowing the joy of the creating and redeeming God himself.

APPENDIX

Books besides the Bible to Use in Discipling Relationships

Sam Allberry. *Is God Anti-Gay? And Other Questions about Homosexuality, the Bible and Same-Sex Attraction*. Purcellville, VA: The Good Book Company, 2013.

Thabiti Anyabwile. *Finding Faithful Elders and Deacons*. Wheaton, IL: Crossway, 2012.

D. A. Carson. *The Difficult Doctrine of the Love of God*. Wheaton, IL: Crossway, 2000.

——. *Praying with Paul: A Call to Spiritual Reformation*. Grand Rapids, MI: Baker Academic, 2014.

Robert Coleman. *The Master Plan of Evangelism*. Grand Rapids, MI: Revell, 1963, 1993.

Mark Dever. *The Gospel and Personal Evangelism*. Wheaton, IL: Crossway, 2007.

——. *What Is a Healthy Church?* Wheaton, IL: Crossway, 2007.

Kevin DeYoung. *Taking God At His Word: Why the Bible Is Knowable, Necessary, and Enough, and What That Means for You and Me*. Wheaton, IL: Crossway, 2014.

———. *Just Do Something: A Liberating Approach to Finding God's Will*. Chicago: Moody, 2009.

Greg Gilbert. *What Is the Gospel?* Wheaton, IL: Crossway, 2010.

David Helm. *One to One Bible Reading: A Simple Guide for Every Christian*. Kingsford: Matthias Media, 2011.

Jonathan Leeman. *Church Membership: How the World Knows Who Represents Jesus*. Wheaton, IL: Crossway, 2012.

———. *Reverberation: How God's Word Brings Light, Freedom, and Action to His People*. Chicago: Moody, 2011.

Carolyn Mahaney. *Feminine Appeal*. Wheaton, IL: Crossway, 2004.

C. J. Mahaney. *Living the Cross-Centered Life: Keeping the Gospel the Main Thing*. Sisters, OR: Multnomah, 2006.

———. *Humility: True Greatness*. Sisters, OR: Multnomah, 2005.

Jason Mandryk. *Operation World: The Definitive Prayer Guide to Every Nation*. Colorado Springs: Biblica, 2010.

Will Metzger. *Tell the Truth: The Whole Gospel Wholly by Grace Communicated Truthfully and Lovingly*. Downers Grove, IL: InterVarsity Press, 1981, 2012.

J. I. Packer. *Concise Theology: A Guide to Historic Christian Beliefs*. Wheaton, IL: Tyndale, 1993.

———. *Evangelism and the Sovereignty of God*. Downers Grove, IL: InterVarsity Press, 1961.

———. *Knowing God*. Downers Grove, IL: InterVarsity Press, 1973.

Richard Phillips. *The Masculine Mandate: God's Calling to Men.* Lake Mary, FL: Reformation Trust, 2009.

John Piper. *God Is the Gospel: Meditations on God's Love as the Gift of Himself.* Wheaton, IL: Crossway, 2005.

———. *Future Grace: The Purifying Power of the Promises of God.* Rev. ed. Colorado Springs: Multnomah, 2012.

———. *The Pleasures of God: Meditations on God's Delight in Being God.* Colorado Springs: Multnomah, 1991, 2000.

Gary Ricucci and Betsy Ricucci. *Love That Lasts: When Marriage Meets Grace.* Wheaton, IL: Crossway, 2006.

Vaughan Roberts. *God's Big Picture: Tracing the Storyline of the Bible.* Downers Grove, IL: InterVarsity Press, 2002.

J. C. Ryle. *A Call to Prayer.* Carlisle, PA: Banner of Truth, 2005.

———. *Holiness.* Abridged ed. Chicago: Moody, 2010.

Orlando Saer. *Big God: How to Approach Suffering, Spread the Gospel, Make Decisions and Pray in the Light of a God Who Really Is in the Driving Seat of the World.* Ross-shire: Christian Focus, 2014.

Richard Sibbes. *The Bruised Reed.* Edinburgh: Banner of Truth, 1998.

R. C. Sproul. *The Holiness of God.* 2nd ed. Wheaton, IL: Tyndale, 1998.

Mack Stiles. *Evangelism: How the Whole World Speaks of Jesus.* Wheaton, IL: Crossway, 2014.

Sebastian Traeger and Greg Gilbert. *The Gospel at Work: How Working for King Jesus Gives Purpose and Meaning to Our Jobs*. Grand Rapids, MI: Zondervan, 2013.

Ed Welch. *When People Are Big and God Is Small: Overcoming Peer Pressure, Codependency, and the Fear of Man*. Phillipsburg, NJ: P&R, 1997.

Don Whitney. *Spiritual Disciplines of the Christian Life*. Rev. ed. Colorado Springs: NavPress, 2014.

NOTES

Introduction

1. Robert D. Putnam, *Bowling Alone: The Collapse and Revival of American Community* (New York: Simon & Schuster, 2000); Sherry Turkle, *Alone Together: Why We Expect More from Technology and Less from Each Other* (New York: Basic Books, 2011); Eric Klinenberg, *Going Solo: The Extraordinary Rise and Surprising Appeal of Living Alone* (New York, Penguin, 2012).

2. Klinenberg, *Going Solo*, 208.

3. Ibid.

4. David F. Wells, *Above All Earthly Pow'rs: Christ in a Postmodern World* (Grand Rapids, MI: Eerdmans, 2005), 119.

Chapter 2: Oriented toward Others

1. Charles Bridges, *The Christian Ministry: With an Inquiry into the Causes of Its Inefficiency* (Carlisle, PA: Banner of Truth, 1959), 75.

Chapter 3: The Work of Discipling

1. Erin Wheeler, "Discipling When You Need to Be Discipled," in *9Marks Journal*, "Discipling in the Church," September–October 2012, http://9marks.org/article/journaldiscipling-when-you-need-be-discipled/.

2. C. H. Spurgeon, *C. H. Spurgeon Autobiography*, vol. 2, *The Full Harvest* (Carlisle, PA: Banner of Truth, 1973), 131.

Chapter 4: Objections to Discipling

1. Alice Fryling, *Disciplemakers' Handbook: Helping People Grow in Christ* (Downers Grove, IL: InterVarsity Press, 1989), 48.

Chapter 9: Pay the Cost

1. Richard Sibbes, "The Bride's Longing," in *Works of Richard Sibbes*, vol. 6, ed. Alexander B. Grosart (Carlisle, PA: Banner of Truth, 1983 ed.), 560.

Chapter 10: Raising Up Leaders

1. Samuel Miller, *Letters on Clerical Manners and Habits: To a Student in the Theological Seminary at Princeton, N.J.*, Applewood's American Philosophy and Religion Series (Bedford, MA: Applewood Books, 1827), 406–7.

2. Henry Drummond, *The Greatest Thing in the World and Other Addresses* (London: Hodder and Stoughton, 1959), 36.

SCRIPTURE INDEX

Deuteronomy
6:6–7   28

2 Samuel
book of   102
23:3–4   102

Psalms
8:5–6   113
25:9   79

Proverbs
11:2   79
27:6   90

Matthew
13:31–32   35
16:13–20   55
18   65
18:15–20   39, 56
20:25–27   101
20:25–28   107
28:18   113
28:18–20   56
28:19   12
28:19–20   17

Mark
3:13–14   29
8:34   15, 74
10:45   27
12:28–31   90
12:30   16
12:31   16

Luke
6:40   25

John
10:11   14
13:34   89
13:34–35   48, 54

13:35   84
14:15   17
14:23   17
15:8–17   84
15:12–14   17

Acts
book of   56
16   29
16:3   29
20   103
20:28   99

Romans
10:17   59
12:2   24
12:10–16   64–65

1 Corinthians
1:5   100
1:7   100
2:14   75
4:15   84
5   65
5:6   25
6:19–20   15
10:17   37, 56
11:1   40, 61, 84
11:26   60
12:4–7   68
12:12–26   64
12:14–15   64
13   54
13:7   97
15:33   25

2 Corinthians
2:6   65
4:7   36, 42

5:15	15	5:1	77
12:9	26	5:8	75
		5:17	63
Galatians			
1:8	64	*2 Timothy*	
4:9	84	1:12	113
6:6	63	2:2	29–30, 51, 79,
6:10	80		93
		3:10–11	84, 85
Ephesians		4:3	63
2:2	24	4:5	59
2:10	80		
2:18	78	*Titus*	
4:11–16	60	1	93
4:29	67	1:5	93
5:16	80	1:6–9	61, 94
5:25	14	2:3–5	77
Philippians		*Hebrews*	
1:12–30	111	book of	75
2:1	14	2:6–8	113
2:15	85	10:24	64, 74
2:16	84	10:24–25	41, 55
2:17	42	13	97
3:17	84, 85	13:7	40, 62, 76
4:9	84	13:17	62, 76
Colossians		*James*	
1:28	74	2:1	95
1:28–29	30		
1:29	30	*1 Peter*	
2:2	32	2:9	43
3:16	41	2:18–20	25
		2:21	39
1 Thessalonians		2:21–25	25
5:11	74	3:1	25
5:12–13	63	4:4	24
5:17	89	5:5	79
2 Thessalonians		*1 John*	
3:7–9	84	4:19–21	17
1 Timothy		*2 John*	
2:14	103	5	74
3	93		
3:1–7	62, 94	*Revelation*	
4:12	77	7:9–10	78
4:16	60, 83	20:6	113

9Marks

Building Healthy Churches

9Marks exists to equip church leaders with a biblical vision and practical resources for displaying God's glory to the nations through healthy churches.

To that end, we want to see churches characterized by these nine marks of health:

1   Expositional Preaching
2   Biblical Theology
3   A Biblical Understanding of the Gospel
4   A Biblical Understanding of Conversion
5   A Biblical Understanding of Evangelism
6   Biblical Church Membership
7   Biblical Church Discipline
8   Biblical Discipleship
9   Biblical Church Leadership

Find all our Crossway titles
and other resources at
www.9Marks.org

9MARKS: BUILDING HEALTHY CHURCHES SERIES

Based on Mark Dever's best-selling book *Nine Marks of a Healthy Church*, each book in this series helps readers grasp basic biblical commands regarding the local church.

TITLES INCLUDE:

Biblical Theology	Conversion	The Gospel
Church Discipline	Discipling	Missions
Church Elders	Evangelism	Prayer
Church Membership	Expositional Preaching	Sound Doctrine

For more information, visit crossway.org.
For translated versions of these and other 9Marks books, visit 9Marks.org/bookstore/translations.